Bread Reflections and
Family Distractions

Bread Reflections and
Family Distractions

Dolores Clark Haggerty

iUniverse, Inc.
New York Lincoln Shanghai

Bread Reflections and *Family Distractions*

iUniverse, Inc.

For information address:
iUniverse, Inc.
2021 Pine Lake Road, Suite 100
Lincoln, NE 68512
www.iuniverse.com

ISBN: 0-595-33021-5

Printed in the United States of America

For
Ethel (1903–1969) and Mary (1902–1987)
Mother and Mother-in-law
They Never Found Fault

Contents

Acknowledgments

Thank you Miriam Shnycer for your ongoing support. Thank you Ruth Hayes for your insightful comments, and my thanks to Joan Sweet for reading the basic bread manuscript.

I am grateful to my husband Ed for his patience and to my children, Edward, Maureen, Daniel and Anna, for their recipe suggestions and bread flavor opinions. Thanks to my grandchildren, Emma, Madeleine and Rebecca for their bread enjoyment.

I owe a debt of gratitude to my Saturday writing group: Maribeau Briggs, Gisela Epple, Sharon Perkins, Tom Reilly and John Shrawder for encouraging me to publish.

Bread Reflections and Family Distractions

This book, "Bread Reflections and *Family Distractions*," encourages bread baking with clearly written recipes, extensive directions, ingredient facts, and suggestions for bread fillings, toppings and meals. Throughout the book are distractions ♥ that came to mind as the bread baked.

How to Use This Bread Book

The Basic white, sweet and dark-bread recipes and directions in Chapters 1, 2 and 3 are for one loaf or five loaves. The time necessary from start to finish for one loaf or for five loaves is two hours. If you have never made bread, begin with the one-loaf recipe. You will appreciate the explicit directions. If you have baked bread before—with poor results—the explicit directions will encourage you to bake bread again. Because the baker should not have to refer back and forth to various pages to bake bread, the ingredients and directions for each Basic recipe—white, sweet and dark—are written in full.

Before you begin to bake bread, look to Chapter 4, Mix, Knead, Bake and Serve, and plan your bread making. After you have baked bread a few times, look to Chapter 5, Ingredients That Change Bread Taste and Texture, and design your bread recipes. The nutritional information—calorie, carbohydrate, fat, protein, sodium and fiber amounts in this chapter are from the U. S. Department of Agriculture Nutritive Value of Foods, Home and Garden Bulletin Number 72 dated 2002, and from individual manufacturer product labels.

In Chapter 6, Tasty Toppings and Wholesome Meals, there are sweet and savory toppings for dough and bread along with recipes for energizing previously baked breads. In Chapter 7—Reflecting on Your Diet, there is additional information relating to bread/nutrition.

Abbreviations

Dozen...doz
Fluid oz...oz
Gallon...gal
Gram...g
Liquid...lq
Milligrams...mg
Pound...lb
Package...pkg
Quart...qt

1

Basic White-Bread Recipe, Directions and Recipe Suggestions

The Basic white bread directions are very detailed, but this is necessary to ensure a golden-brown and delicious tasting loaf. If you are new at bread baking, and have questions about Baking Area etc. then look to Chapter 4—Mix, Knead, Bake and Serve.

Before starting to bake bread, read through the directions, warm the immediate baking area, and set out utensils and ingredients. (Refer to Baking area, Oven, Time and Utensils in Chapter 4.)

Basic White-Bread Recipe and Directions for One Loaf and Five Loaves

Baking Area
Area to knead dough (counter top/or table top) should be at least—24" x 34". Area to Rest/Rise dough should be close to 80°. It is all right if baking area is not exactly 80°.

Oven
Preheat oven to 350°

Time
Bake 40 minutes

Utensils
Measuring cups
Measuring spoons

Mixing spoon
Knife to level flour
Container to mix ingredients
Pot to heat liquid
Liquid thermometer
Room thermometer
Lightly oiled 8 ½" x 4 ½" bread pan
Rolling pin—optional
Cooling rack

♦Because it packs the flour too densely, do not dip aluminum measuring cup into flour bag. Rather, place the cup on a plate or wax paper and spoon or pour from flour bag into the cup. Use a level measuring cup, and level flour with the straight side of a knife. Return the spilled over flour back into the flour container.

Basic White-Bread Recipe

Ingredients for Basic white bread—one loaf or five loaves
One Loaf
4-cups all-purpose white flour
1-pk dry yeast
2-teaspoons salt
1-tablespoon sugar
1-cup water
½-cup whole milk
2-tablespoons vegetable oil

Five Loaves
20-cups all-purpose white flour
4-pkgs dry yeast
2-tablespoons salt
¼-cup sugar
4-cups water
2-cups whole milk
½-cup vegetable oil

Directions for Basic white bread—one loaf or five loaves
1—**Hold aside flour to use later**. For the one-loaf recipe, hold aside ½ cup flour. For the five-loaf recipe, hold aside 1-cup flour. Otherwise, the directions are the same for one loaf or five loaves.

2—**Container**—With a large spoon, mix the remaining flour, yeast, salt and sugar for about one minute.

3—**Pot**—On medium heat, warm the liquid: water, milk and vegetable oil. When thermometer reads 130° remove liquid from the heat.
It is all right if the thermometer reads degree more or less.

4—All at once pour liquid into the container with the dry ingredients, blend with a large spoon and then gather together with your hands.

5—**Kneading dough**
   A. While in the container, gather the blended dough into a round.
       The dough might seem dry, but this will change with kneading.
   B. On a flat surface, sprinkle 1-tablespoon of the set aside flour.
   C. Turn dough from the container, and rub flour from your hands and from inside the container.
   D. Flatten dough slightly then fold the dough.
   E. Press folded dough down firmly with the heel of your hands.
   F. Turn dough about one quarter around.
   G. Repeat flatten, fold, press firmly and turn dough.
   H. If dough sticks to the flat surface, add 1-tablespoon of the set aside flour as needed.
   I. Continue to flatten, fold, press and turn the dough for ten minutes.
   You have completed kneading.

6—**Resting dough**—Cover dough with a towel, and allow dough to rest for fifteen minutes in 80° baking area.

7—After fifteen minutes, the dough will rise and be too awkward to work with. Press dough down in a few places to release the air.

(If you follow the recipe for five loaves, now is the time to divide the dough into five loaves. Five 8 ½" x 4 ½" bread pans fit into most kitchen ovens.)

(This is the Basic white-bread recipe dough called for in the following recipes—Bread Sticks, Pizza, Pretzels etc.)

8—**Shaping dough**—Use your hands/fingers or rolling pin to flatten dough to about 8" x 12". Firmly roll up dough; tuck in ends and place seam side down into a lightly oiled 8 ½" x 4 ½" baking pan. If you have left over flour, save it for the next time you bake bread.

9—**Rising dough**—Cover dough with a light towel, and set in 80° baking area to rise for 40 minutes.

10—Use a serrated knife to slash 1/16 inch down the loaf, or three /// slashes across the loaf. This encourages dough to bake evenly. (Refer to Slash /// in Chapter 4)

11—Bake 350° for 40 minutes. Remove golden brown bread from the pan, and cool on a cooling rack.

12—Take time to applaud your efforts.

One-Loaf Suggestions Basic White Dough

After the Basic white dough is raised (step #7), you can follow through and bake the bread or you can add ingredients. Shown below are a few one-loaf recipe suggestions for Basis white dough—

American Bread, Braided Bread, Bread Sticks, Cheese Bread, Dinner Rolls, Fried Bread, Hard Crusted White Round, Hot Dog Wrap, Long Loaves, Pepperoni Bread, Pizza, Pizza Bread, Pretzels and Spice Bread

American Bread

The Basic white bread recipe in this book is for American Bread—one loaf or five loaves. For sure American bread is the all time favorite: fresh for slicing, day old for sandwiches, three days old for toast, stuffing etc.

After the Basic white bread is baked, slice and lather with butter. One bite will jog your memory to a time when American bread had taste and texture.

♥ *Early 1950s—My introduction to homemade American bread was at a high school friend's house. When my friend opened the front door to her home, bread aroma greeted me. When she removed the bread from the oven it was too brown, and she apologized. For my part, her efforts were impressive. We broke apart the crusty loaf, and lathered warm bread with cold butter.*

♥ *Early 1950s—I traveled to and from high school on the Frankford elevated train, which passed along side the upper floors of the Bond Bread Bakery. On a dreary winter day the factory lights reflected a golden glow onto the bakers and the ovens. The bread-baking aroma permeated the neighborhood.*

Braided Bread
Oven—preheat to 350°
Time—40 minutes
Utensils—oiled baking sheet, cooling rack
Ingredients—Basic white-bread recipe dough, 2-tablespoons flour for counter top, 1-fork beaten egg

1—Divide dough into three pieces and roll into three—12" lengths.
2—Set side by side on baking sheet.
3—Braid dough from the middle, pinch ends together and turn under.
4—Cover with a light towel and let rise for 40 minute.
5—Lightly brush dough with egg.
6—Bake 40 minutes 350°.
7—Immediately remove from pan to cooling rack.
Place the baked loaf in a breadbasket with a colorful napkin.
This braided loaf can also be baked in an 8 ½" x 4 ½" pan.

♥*August 19ᵗʰ 2000—I gave my granddaughter Madeleine a slice of buttered sweet bread. And, she questioned, "Why does the bread taste different?" I said, "I gave you sweet bread." Madeleine handed back the bread and requested the more familiar white bread.*

Bread Sticks
Oven—preheat to 350°
Time—30 minutes
Utensils—oiled baking sheet, cooling rack
Ingredients—Basic white-bread recipe dough, 2-tablespoons flour for counter top, ¼ cup sesame seeds or poppy seeds, 2 fork beaten egg whites

1—Cut dough into 30-tablespoon size pieces.
2—Roll each piece into a pencil long strip, brush with egg white and sprinkle on seeds.
(The egg white keeps the seeds from popping off as dough bakes.)
3—Place on an oiled baking sheet, cover and let rise for 20 minutes.
4—Bake 30 minutes 350°.
5—Immediately turn bread sticks onto a cooling rack.
Homemade bread sticks are a fun change from everyday sliced bread, and are great served with soup. They are delicious sprinkled with coarse salt.

Bread Sticks—Cheese

Knead 1-tablespoon Italian spice and 1-cup cheese into Basic white-dough.
Follow directions for bread sticks.
Serve bread sticks with warm olive oil and fresh herbs.

Bread Sticks—Cinnamon

Sprinkle dough with ¼-cup white sugar blended with 1-tablespoon cinnamon.
Follow directions for bread sticks.

Cheese Bread

Oven—preheat to 350°
Time—40 minutes
Utensils—oiled bread pan 8 ½" x 4 ½", cooling rack
Ingredients—Basic white-bread recipe dough, 2-tablespoons flour for counter top, 1-cup grated sharp cheese

1—Knead cheese into dough for about 2 minutes.
2—Flatten dough to 10" x 8", roll and tuck in ends.
3—Place in baking pan, cover and allow dough to rise for 40 minutes.
4—Make slash /// across the top. Bake 40 minutes 350°.
5—Immediately remove from pan to cooling rack.
Enjoy a cheese bread sandwich.

Dinner Rolls

Oven—preheat to 350°
Time—40 minutes
Utensils—oiled 9" cake pan, medium size circular roll cutter, cooling rack
Ingredients—Basic white-bread recipe dough, 2-tablespoons flour for counter top

1—Flatten dough into a round.
2—Cut dough into 10–12 rounds and place side by side in baking pan.
3—Cover and allow dough to rise 20 minutes.
4—Bake for 30–40 minutes 350°.
5—Immediately remove from pan to cooling rack.
For sandwich rolls cut dough into 8 pieces and bake on baking sheet with dough sides not touching.

♥ *Mid and late 1960s—When I first started to make bread, my mother and mother-in-law encouraged my bread baking efforts. They had comments to make about each, loaf, slice and mouthful. Their comments were put to use, and are reflected throughout this bread book.*

FriedBread

Utensils—Deep fryer, slotted spoon, knife, paper towel, cooling rack
Ingredients—Basic white-bread recipe dough, 2-tablespoons flour for counter top, oil, salt, pepper, powder sugar

1—Cut dough into 30 tablespoon size pieces and allow to rise 30 minutes.
2—Deep fry—Heat oil according to deep fry directions.
3—Place some dough pieces into hot oil; bread will rise to top when ready.
4—When brown, remove dough and place on a paper towel.
5—Sprinkle hot dough with salt and pepper or powder sugar.
For full flavor, eat this fun snack immediately.
After use, pour the oil into a container, cover tight and refrigerate for next use.

♥ *Early 1970s—We visited with friends Peggy and Jerry who helped the children make fried bread Italian style—a fun-filled afternoon.*
I met Peggy and Jerry when Ed and Jerry worked for Radio Corporation of America (RCA) Early Warning Radar System in Yorkshire, England.

Hard Crusted White Round
Oven—preheat to 400° and then 350°
Time—40 minutes—bake bread for 10 minutes @ 400°and 30 minutes @ 350°
Utensil—oiled baking sheet, cooling rack
Ingredients—Basic white-bread recipe dough, 2-tablespoons flour for counter top, 2-tablespoons cornmeal

1—Flatten dough into a round.
2—Sprinkle corn meal onto baking sheet, and place dough on baking sheet.
4—Cover and allow dough to rise for 40 minutes.
5—Make slash /// across the top. Bake 400° for 10 minutes.
6—Set oven temperature to 350° and bake for 30 more minutes.
7—Immediately remove bread from pan to a cooling rack.
Blend 1-clove crushed garlic with 2-tablespoons fresh herbs and 2-tablespoons olive oil.
Serve warm with hard crusted white bread and aged cheese.

♥ *Early 1990s—On a visit with cousin Margie in Charlotte, NC, Wilson, Margie's husband, baked delicious crusty white bread Italian style.*

Hot Dog Wraps
Oven—preheat to 350°
Time—30–40 minutes
Utensils—oiled baking sheet, rolling pin, knife, cooling rack
Ingredients—Basic white-bread recipe dough, 2-tablespoons flour for counter top, 8 hot dogs, 8 cheese slices, ¼-cup water

1—Flatten dough and cut into 8 squares.
(Or cut dough into strips and wrap 16 hot dogs.)
2—Cut hot dogs lengthwise and insert folded cheese.
3—Wrap dough around hot dogs and pinch dough together with few drops water.
4—Cover and allow dough to rise 30 minutes. Bake 30–40 minutes.
This variation on hot dog rolls is a family favorite. Serve with canned baked beans that have been doctored to taste with catsup, mustard and brown sugar.

♥ *1949—MY first employment was at the Philadelphia Zoo selling hot dogs and sodas. The pay was $4.00, less tax for a days work.*

Long Loaf

Oven—preheat to 400° then 350°

Time—For crisp loaf, bake bread 20 minutes @ 400° and 20 minutes @ 350°

Utensils—oiled baking sheet, pastry brush, small pan with water, cooling rack

Ingredients—Basic white-bread recipe dough, 2-tablespoons flour for counter top, 2-tablespoons corn meal, cold water

1—Oil a baking sheet and sprinkle with corn meal.

2—Roll and pull dough from center until dough is length of baking sheet.

3—Place on baking sheet. Cover.

4—Let rise for 40 minutes. With a serrated knife cut three lines /// across loaf.

5—In bottom rack of preheated oven, place small pan water.

When hot, the water will circulate steam inside oven and give bread a crisp crust.

6—Brush dough with cold water and bake 400° for 20 minutes.

7—After 20 minutes, again brush dough with cold water, and bake for 20 minutes longer at 350°.

8—Immediately remove bread from pan to cooling rack.

This long loaf is reminiscent of European bread with hearty goodness of the Basic white bread.

♥ *October 1st 1988—We modernize the Medford Lakes kitchen to include a magnificent self-cleaning, eye level oven. An oven that works properly! I immediately baked two long loaves of bread.*

Pepperoni Bread

Oven—preheat to 350°
Time—40 minutes
Utensil—oiled 8 ½" x 4 ½" pan, rolling pin, cooling rack
Ingredients—Basic white-bread recipe dough, 2-tablespoons flour for counter top, 1-cup pepperoni cut into small pieces

1—Flatten the dough to about 8" x 12"
2—Distribute pepperoni onto dough.
3—Roll dough, and tuck ends.
4—Place the dough seam side down into bread pan.
5—Cover and allow dough to rise for 40 minutes.
6—Make slash /// across the top.
7—Bake 40 minutes—350°. Immediately remove from pan to cooling rack.
Slice this bread for cheese sandwiches or braid the dough for party snacking.

♥ *1970s and 1980s—Through grade school and high school Edward and Daniel, and their friends used the kitchen table to play cards, war games or Dungeons and Dragons. Although the boys were annoyed if other family members bothered them, they tolerated the baker and enjoyed pepperoni bread.*

Pizza

Oven—preheat to 350°

Time—30 minutes

Utensils—oiled pizza pan, cheese grater, spoon, sharp knife

Ingredients—½ Basic white-bread recipe dough, 2-tablespoons flour for counter top, 1-½ cups tomato sauce, 1-cup mozzarella cheese, 1-teaspoon Italian spice, 1-tablespoon olive oil

1—Flatten the dough until it covers the pizza pan.

If you have trouble with the dough, let the dough set 15 minutes in 80° area.

2—Spread sauce, sprinkle cheese, add spices then dot with olive oil.

3—Cover and allow dough to rise 30 minutes.

4—Bake at 350° for 30 minutes.

For a thick crust, use the full Basic white-bread recipe dough and bake 40 minutes.

For a selection of pizza toppings see Tasty toppings in Chapter 6.

Pizza—dough, sauce, cheese and spice—continues to be a sought after food. The reason is fresh-baked crust. Some folks prefer thin crust—enough to hold sauce and cheese. Others folks prefer thick crust—enough to hold sauce, cheese, meat and vegetables. But all prefer a restaurant/home where the crust is fresh baked

♥ *On November 13th 2003—I had lunch with Leane, a friend from my days as a social worker. While we discussed daughter Evelyn, who was born in August, daughter Cara, at age three, entertained, herself with the small cheese shaker. Cara slowly shook out a few grains of cheese onto the table, and with moist fingers took up the grains, and evaluated them. She then placed her fingers into her mouth where more evaluation took place. She repeated this, and repeated this, and....*

Pizza Bread

Oven—preheat to 350°

Time—40 minutes

Utensil—oiled 8 ½" x 4 ½" pan, rolling pin, cheese grater, spoon, sharp knife, cooling rack

Ingredients—Basic white-bread recipe dough, 2-tablespoons flour for counter top, 1-cup tomato sauce, ½ cup grated mozzarella cheese and 1-teaspoon Italian spice

The temptation is to add additional sauce, but too much sauce will ooze out of the dough onto the pan.

1—Roll the dough to about 8" x 12".

2—Distribute tomato sauce, sprinkle on cheese and the spice.

3—Roll dough, and tuck ends so the sauce has no escape.

4—Place the dough seam side down into an oiled bread pan.

5—Cover and allow dough to rise for 40 minutes.

6—Make slash /// across the top.

7—Bake 40 minutes—350°.

8—Immediately remove from pan to cooling rack.

Pizza bread is fast food, party food and nutritious food.

♥*Early 1950s—On Saturday nights, my high school friends and I enjoyed 'Tomato Pie' at a 'pizza parlor 'located at 49th and Lancaster Avenue—hot crusty pizza with spicy tomato sauce. This tomato pie (not called pizza in the fifties) was served hot from the oven without cheese.*

♥*March 16th 1968—In a letter to her sister Rachel, my mother informed Rachel, "Dolores has been making her own bread. She uses dry yeast. The bread taste very good." (My mother always thought today more important than yesterday and seldom reminisced. But neither my mother nor her sister ever threw away letters. In 2001 Rachel's son Ralph gave this letter and other letters to me.)*

♥*Late 1970s—While making pizza bread, Maureen and I had fun experimenting with pizza dough, and used more tomato sauce than the dough could hold. While rolling the white dough, the red sauce spilled onto hands and counter. A mess. To resolve this, Maureen suggested that, next time, we should serve the extra sauce in a side dish.*

Pretzels

Oven—preheat to 350°
Time—30 minutes
Utensil—oiled baking sheet, cooling rack
Ingredients—Basic white-bread recipe dough, 2-tablespoons flour for counter top, fork beaten egg white, coarse salt

1—Flatten the dough and cut into 10 pieces.
2—Roll each piece 12" long, and shape into pretzel.
(Take each end in hand, curve and cross over.)
3—Brush with egg white and sprinkle with coarse salt.
4—Cover and allow dough to rise for 30 minutes.
5—Bake 350° for 30 minutes. Immediately remove from pan to cooling rack.
Pretzels are also tasty when made with Basic sweet-recipe dough.

♥ *1940–1948—While I attended St. Gregory's grade school, soft pretzels were served every day during school recess. Pretzels were a delicious, satisfying and inexpensive snack, and when covered with mustard they found favor with boys and girls in every grade.*

♥ *2000—If you scan the pretzel selection in any supermarket, you know the folks from Philadelphia area consume the most pretzel products—soft, hard, long, round, flat, mini, chocolate, cheese, peanut butter etc.*

Spice Bread
 Oven—preheat to 350°
 Time—40 minutes
 Utensils—oiled bread pan 8 ½" x 4 ½", cooling rack
 Ingredients—Basic white-bread recipe dough, 2-tablespoons flour for counter top, ½ teaspoon oregano, ½ teaspoon hot pepper, ¼ cup dry tomato—cut small, ½ cup locatelli cheese.

 1—Flatten dough, sprinkle on ingredients and knead for about 2 minutes.
 2—Flatten dough 10" x 8", roll and tuck in ends.
 3—Place in baking pan, cover and allow dough to rise for 40 minutes.
 (When using hot pepper, do not rub your eyes.
 And wash your hands and work area to remove the hot pepper.)
 4—Make slash /// across the top.
 5—Bake 40 minutes 350°. Immediately remove from pan to cooling rack.
 Those of us who avoid high spice might avoid this recipe.

♥*December 28ᵗʰ, 1993—I originally planned to make bread sticks for a holiday party, but I have little patience for making so many sticks, and made tasty spice bread.*

Home-Made Bread—Warmth, Friendship, Togetherness, Love

2

Basic Sweet-Bread Recipe, Directions and Recipe Suggestions

Basic sweet bread has a pleasant taste, fine texture and rich color. The aroma, on a winter morning, ensures that sleepy family members will enter the kitchen with a smile.

Before starting to bake bread, read through the directions, warm the immediate baking area, and set out utensils and ingredients. (Refer to Baking area, Oven, Time and Utensils in Chapter 4.)

Basic Sweet-Bread Recipe and Directions for One Loaf and Five Loaves

Baking Area
Area to knead dough (counter top/or table top) should be at least—24" x 34".
Area to Rest/Rise dough should be close to 80°. It is all right if area is not exactly 80°.

Oven
Preheat oven to 350°

Time
Bake 40 minutes

Utensils
Measuring cups
Measuring spoons
Mixing spoon
Knife to level flour

Container to mix ingredients
Pot to heat liquid
Bowl and fork to mix egg
Liquid thermometer
Room thermometer
Lightly oiled 8 ½" x 4 ½" Bread Pan
Rolling pin—optional
Cooling rack

♦Because it packs the flour too densely, do not dip aluminum measuring cup into flour bag. Rather, place the cup on a plate or wax paper and spoon or pour from flour bag into the cup. Use a level measuring cup, and level flour with the straight side of a knife. Return the spilled over flour back into the flour container.

Basic Sweet-Bread Recipe

Ingredients for Basic sweet bread—one loaf or five loaves
One Loaf
4-cups all-purpose white flour
1-pk dry yeast
2-teaspoons salt
3-tablespoons sugar
¾-cup water
½-cup whole milk
2-tablespoons vegetable oil
1-fork beaten egg

Five Loaves
20-cups all-purpose white flour
4-pkgs dry yeast
2-tablespoons salt
1-cup sugar
3-cups water
2-cups whole milk
½-cup vegetable oil
4-fork beaten eggs

Directions for Basic sweet bread—one loaf or five loaves

1—Hold aside flour to use later. For the one-loaf recipe, hold aside ½ cup flour. For the five-loaf recipe, hold aside 1-cup flour. Otherwise, the directions are the same for one loaf or five loaves.

2—**Container**—With a large spoon, mix the remaining flour, yeast, salt and sugar for about one minute.

3—**Pot**—On medium heat warm the water, milk, vegetable oil **<Not The Eggs>.**
When temperature reaches 130°, remove liquid from the heat.
It is all right if the thermometer reads a degree more or less.

4—All at once pour warm liquid into the container with the dry ingredients, and blend with a large spoon. (If you have questions see mixing eggs in Chapter 4.)

5—Add fork-beaten—room temperature—egg and continue to blend mixture.

6—When ingredients are too dense to mix with a spoon, gather together with your hands.
The dough might seem dry, but this will change with kneading.

7—Kneading

   A. On a flat surface sprinkle 1-tablespoon set aside flour.
   B. Turn dough mixture from pan onto floured surface.
   C. Gather dough together into a round, and include bits and pieces from pan.
   D. Flatten dough slightly.
   E. Fold dough in half.
   F. Press folded dough down with the heel of your hands.
   G. Turn dough one quarter around.
   H. Repeat—flatten, fold, press firmly, and turn.
If dough sticks to flat surface add 1-tablespoon set aside flour as needed.
   I. Continue kneading for 10 minutes: flatten, fold, press and turn.
You have completed the kneading section of this recipe.

8—**Resting dough**—Cover dough with a light towel, and allow dough to rest for fifteen minutes in an 80° baking area. (If you have questions about rest/rising dough refer to Chapter 4.)

9—After fifteen minutes, dough will rise and be too awkward to work with. Press dough in a few places with your fist to release the air.

(If you follow the recipe for five loaves, now is the time to divide the dough into five loaves. Five 8 ½" x 4 ½" pans or ten 5" x 3" will fit into most kitchen ovens.)

(This is the Basic sweet bread recipe dough called for in the following recipes—Bowknots, Children's Play, Hot Cross Buns etc.)

10—**Shaping dough**—With your hands or a rolling pin, flatten dough to about 8" x 12". Firmly roll up dough; tuck in ends, and place seam side down in bake pan.
There might be flour left over, this is all right. Use it the next time you bake bread.

11—**Rising dough**—Cover dough with a light towel, and allow dough to rise in an 80° area for 40 minutes. Dough will raise more when placed into hot oven.

12—With a sharp knife make a 1/16 inch slash down loaf, or /// across loaf. This encourages dough to bake evenly. (See Slash /// in Chapter 4.)

13—Preheat oven to 350° and bake 40 minutes. Bread will bake golden brown.

14—Immediately remove bread from pan to cooling rack, and take a photograph of your lovely finished product.

One-Loaf Suggestions Basic Sweet Dough

After the Basic sweet bread is raised (step #9), you can follow through and place the dough into the bread pan or you can add ingredients. Shown below are a few suggestions for Basic sweet dough-

Anna Bevan's Bow Knots, Anna's Cinnamon Pull Apart, Aunt Grace's Saffron Buns, Brown Sugar and Walnut Madness, Children's Play, Daniel's Light Honey Pecan Buns, Edward's Cinnamon Sweet, Ethel's Philadelphia Cinnamon Buns, Hot Cross Buns, Jim's Coconut/Almond Choice, Mame's Holiday Sweet Braid, Maureen's Peanut Butter Bread, Mother's Sweet-Raisin Memory, Nuts and Golden Raisins, Nutty Mincemeat, Prune Bread, and recipe for Five Loaf Favorites

Anna Bevan's Bow Knots

Oven—preheat to 350°
Time—30 minutes
Utensils—oiled bake sheet, rolling pin, knife, cooling rack
Ingredients—Basic sweet bread-recipe dough, 2 tablespoons flour for counter, powder sugar for dusting

1—With a rolling pin, flatten dough to about 8" x 16".
2—Cut dough into strips about 5" long and 1" wide.
3—Tie the strips into knots, and allow dough to rise for 30 minutes.
4—Bake for 30 minutes at 350°.
5—Immediately remove bread from pan to cooling rack.
Cool on a cooling rack and sprinkle with powder sugar.

Bow Knot experiments—

Before baking, brush dough strips with fork beaten egg and sprinkle with granulated sugar.

Or, after baking bowknots, sprinkle with old-fashion vanilla sugar—1-cup sugar—in which split vanilla bean and seeds have been placed for a week or longer.

Or, after baking, drizzle baked bowknots with mixture ½ cup powder sugar mixed with 1-tablespoon water, ½ teaspoon vanilla.

Or, after baking bowknots, brush the tops with melted butter and sprinkle with granulated sugar.

♥ *Early 1900s—My mother said that her mother made Bow Knots to serve with tea to her friends in the small front parlor. And that there were always enough Bow Knots to keep the children: John, Philip, Ethel, Rachel and Thomas in the kitchen.*

Anna's Cinnamon Pull Apart
    Oven—preheat to 350°
    Time—40 minutes
    Utensils—oiled tube pan, knife, cooling rack
    Ingredients—Basic sweet-bread recipe dough, 2-tablespoons flour for counter top, ½-cup soft butter, cinnamon mix—1-tablespoon cinnamon with ¼-cup sugar

    1—Cut dough into 30 pieces. Dip each piece into soft butter then cinnamon sugar mixture.
    2—Place butter/sugar dough pieces into the tube pan.
    3—Cover and allow dough to rise for 40 minutes.
    3—Bake for 40 minutes at 350°.
    4—Immediately remove bread from pan to a cooling rack.
    This bread has a delicious cinnamon-sweet flavor, wonderful aroma and it is fun to pull apart.

♥ *Early 1970s—When in grade school, my daughter Anna could be heard to exclaim, "I am not getting up; I am not going to school." But if she awoke to bread aroma, there was seldom a problem.*

Aunt Grace's Saffron Buns
Oven—preheat to 350°
Time—40 minutes
Utensils—oiled 10" x 10" baking pan, cooling rack
Ingredients—Basic sweet-bread recipe dough, 2-tablespoons flour for counter top, a few strands of saffron

1—Knead saffron into dough.
2—Flatten dough 8" x 16", firmly roll up dough and slice.
3—Place in pan, cover and allow dough to rise for 40 minutes.
4—Bake for 40 minutes—350°. Immediately remove bread from pan to cooling rack.
Saffron colors dough yellow, and has indescribable flavor. For additional texture and flavor, add glazed fruit, nuts or raisins.

♥ *December 25ᵗʰ 1980—Each holiday Grace, Ed's brother Joe's wife, baked exotic tasting saffron buns, and then brought the buns and other goodies to the holiday celebration.*

♥ *Because Grace's mother made delicious bread, Grace had bread-baking memories. Grace said, "My father referred to store-purchased bread and rolls as, 'Belly Poison'."*

Brown Sugar/Walnut Madness
Oven—preheat to 350°
Time—40 minutes
Utensils—9" cake pan, cooling rack
Ingredients—Basic sweet-bread recipe dough, 2-tablespoons flour for counter top, 1-cup chopped walnuts, ½-cup brown sugar, 3-tablespoons soft butter

1—Flatten dough with rolling pin or your fingers to about 8" x 16".
2—Spread butter on dough and sprinkle on brown sugar and nuts.
3—Firmly roll up dough and cut into 12 slices and place in pan.
4—Cover and allow dough to rise for 40 minutes.
5—Bake 40 minutes—350°. Immediately remove bread from pan to cooling rack.
For different madness, follow this recipe and bake as a loaf.

Children's Play

Oven—preheat to 350°
Time—30 minutes
Utensils—oiled bake sheets or cup cake pans, children's utensils, brush, rolling pin, cooling rack etc.
Ingredients—Basic sweet-bread recipe dough, 2-tablespoons flour for table-top, selection of sugar, spice, soft butter, raisins, nuts, peanut butter, jelly, icing drizzle—1-cup sugar, 1 ½-tablespoons milk, drop food color, imagination

1—Divide dough between the children.
2—Roll and slice, flatten and spice, brush with butter.
3—Set in pan, cover and let set 20–30 minutes.
4—Bake 350° for 30–40 minutes or according to imagination size.
5—Immediately turn goodies onto a cooling rack.
There are special utensils for children's play: spatula, whisk, pans etc.

♥ Children's Play has provided entertainment for my children and my grandchildren and many restful moments for myself.

♥ *When designing' with dough and sweet additions—cinnamon, sugar, butter, raisins etc., children follow their heart. The results are different looking—the taste is just fine.*

Daniel's Honey/Pecan Buns

Oven—preheat to 350°
Time—40 minutes
Utensils—oiled 9" cake pan, rolling pin, cooling rack
Ingredients—Basic sweet-bread recipe dough, 2-tablespoons flour for counter top, 3-tablespoons soft butter, 1-cup chopped pecans and ½-cup honey

1—With the rolling pin flatten dough to about 8" x 16".
2—Spread with soft butter and sprinkle on pecans.
3—Firmly roll up dough and cut into 12 slices.
4—Put honey into pan, and place dough slices atop honey.
5—Cover and allow dough to rise for 40 minutes.
6—Bake for 40 minutes—350°.
7—Immediately remove bread from pan to cooling rack.
This is a honey of a bun, and honey is a natural sweetener.

♥ *1981 Stakeout—While I prepared bread in the Medford Lakes kitchen, the Federal Police took up residence in the laundry room adjacent to the kitchen. They wanted to have clear view from the laundry-room window and ready access to the questionable activity in the house across the driveway. On the morning of the stakeout, Daniel had walked to the local woods for shooting. He returned home while the police were in the laundry room. They did not take kindly to his gun. And Dan, age 14 years, did not take kindly to police giving him the third degree for walking around with his BB gun.*
Although they confiscated his gun, they returned it the same evening.

Edward's Cinnamon Sweet
Oven—preheat to 350°
Time—40 minutes
Utensils—oiled 10"x 10" pan, rolling pin, pastry brush, cooling rack
Ingredients—Basic sweet-bread recipe dough, 2-tablespoons flour for counter top, 3 tablespoons soft butter, 1-tablespoon cinnamon mixed with ¼-cup sugar

1—Flatten dough to about 8" x 16".
2—Brush dough with soft butter and sprinkle with cinnamon/sugar mixture.
3—Firmly roll up dough, cut inch wide buns and place side by side in pan.
4—Cover dough and allow 40 minutes to rise. Bake for 40 minutes—350°.
5—Immediately remove buns from pan onto a cooling rack.
For just enough sweetness, sprinkle powder sugar onto baked buns.
For extra sweetness drizzle with icing—mix 1-cup powder sugar with 2-tablespoons milk.

This cinnamon bread burst with goodness when shaped as a loaf and baked in 8 ½" x 4 ½" pan.

♥ *Late 1970s and early 1980s—While attending high school, Edward also attended the U. S. Army Reserves and did Basic training at Fort Dix, NJ. After he graduated high school, he was stationed at Fort Sill, OK where he trained with officers from throughout the world. To his amazement, as 1ˢᵗ Lieutenant he found first-class treatment: good food, and accommodations. For a holiday home visit Edward invited a young man from Turkey to visit New Jersey. After spending a few days at our home, and enjoying home-baked bread, this young man informed me, "Your daughters are too opinionated and they have too much freedom."*

Moreover, each time that I (not Ed) expressed my opinion on a situation or event, the young man would talk over my conversation to discuss his opinion. Needless to say, when the young man returned to military base, my family had good fun following this example.

Ethel's Philadelphia Sticky Cinnamon Buns

Oven—preheat to 350°

Time—40 minutes

Utensils—two-quart stovetop pot, 10" x 10" pan or similar size heavy baking pan with high sides, rolling pin, pastry brush, cooling rack

Ingredients: Topping: 1/3-cup butter, 1/3-cup packed light brown sugar, and 1/3-cup light corn syrup, 1-cup pecans,

Dough: Basic sweet-bread recipe dough

Filling: 1-tablespoon cinnamon mixed with ¼-cup white sugar, 2-tablespoons soft butter, 1-cup raisins

Assemble

1—In the stovetop pot melt butter then blend in corn syrup and brown sugar.

2—Bring mixture to boil then reduce heat and cook for two minutes on medium heat.

3—Spread mixture onto bake pan, place nuts on mixture.

4—Lightly oil the sides of the pan. The light oil helps to keep the dough from sticking and from becoming too dry.

5—Set aside to cool.

Dough

1—Flatten the Basic sweet-bread dough to about 8" x 16".

2—With a pastry brush cover dough with soft butter, cinnamon/sugar mixture and raisins.

Roll and Bake

1—Firmly roll up dough (like a jelly roll). If dough shrinks after rolling, pull a bit from the middle.

2—Cut into one-inch slices and place on melted sugar mixture.

3—Cover dough and allow dough to rise for 40 minutes.

4—Bake 30–40 minutes—350°.

5—Allow buns to rest in pan for 3–5 minutes then turn upright onto a cooling rack.

6—Some sweet liquid will spill onto counter; while hot use a spatula to replace atop baked buns.

When baking Cinnamon buns for a crowd, triple the recipe and bake forty buns in 12" x 17" pan.

This recipe has been followed for a church breakfast, a teacher's get together, a work brunch etc., and, of course, many times for family. The appreciation shown for this fun endeavor will amaze you. I follow this recipe, when teaching bread baking, and all go home with a few cinnamon buns.

♥ *1940s and 1950s—Each Friday, my mother purchased Philadelphia Cinnamon Buns on her way home from work as a seamstress with the U. S. Marine Supply Depot. The cinnamon buns were more than buns with cinnamon. The just-made buns had a sticky brown sugar-butter topping covered with raisins and nuts and just the right cinnamon sweet flavor.*

♥ *During 1960s and 1970s—I had a fun-time finding the exact ingredients and the accurate amounts to fill my cinnamon bun memory. But, if the cinnamon bun experiments did not measure up to expectations, the agreeable taste filled my children's and their friends' expectations—never leftovers.*

♥ *On Saturday, November 8th 2004—A baking student followed the directions for Ethel's Cinnamon Buns and placed the buns into the oven. When he went to retrieve the buns from the oven, he found that although he had the oven on earlier in the day, to warm the baking area, he had forgot to turn the oven back on to bake the buns. He immediately called the Help telephone number, and my husband (who has never baked bread let alone cinnamon buns) answered the telephone. Ed suggested, "Remove the cinnamon buns from the oven, heat the oven to 350° and return cinnamon buns to the oven for baking."*
The student called later in the day to say the buns were delicious.

Hot Cross Buns

Oven—preheat to 350°

Time—40 minutes

Utensils—oiled 10" x 10" baking pan, rolling pin, cooling rack

Ingredients—Basic sweet-bread recipe dough, 2-tablespoons flour for counter top, ½-cup currants, sugar icing: 1-cup powder sugar, 2-tablespoons soft butter, 1-tablespoon milk

1—Knead currants into dough.

2—Flatten dough and cut into 10–12 squares.

3—Place side by side in pan.

4—Cover and allow dough to rise for 40 minutes.

5—Bake 40 minutes—350°. Immediately remove buns from pan to cooling rack.

6—When cool cover buns with a sugar-icing cross.

This is a treat for those who avoid sweets—Ash Wednesday to Easter Sunday.

♥ *1600s—Hot Cross Buns—buns with a white sugar cross are eaten on Shrove Tuesday—the day before Ash Wednesday. Hot cross buns are referred to in a 17ᵗʰ Century Mother-Goose nursery rhyme—"One a penny, two a penny, hot cross buns; if you have no daughters, give them to your sons."*

Jim's Coconut/Almond Bread
    Oven—preheat to 350°
    Time—40 minutes
    Utensils—oiled baking sheet, cooling rack
    Ingredients—Basic sweet-bread recipe dough, 2-tablespoons flour for counter top, 3 tablespoons soft butter, 1-cup sweet coconut, ½-cup chopped almonds

    1—Flatten dough with your fingers to about 8" x 16" and brush with soft butter.
    2—Distribute coconut and almonds onto dough.
    3—Firmly roll up dough and tuck in the ends.
    4—Place dough on a bake sheet.
    5—Make slash /// across the top.
    6—Cover and allow dough to rise for 40 minutes.
    7—Bake 40 minutes—350°. Immediately remove bread from pan to cooling rack.
    This sweet has a delicious chewy crunch.
    Cool and drizzle loaf with lemon icing: 1-cup powder sugar, juice ½-lemon.

♥ *Early 1990s—My son-in-law Jim found Coconut/Almond bread to be his choice and made nice comments. A baker always remembers a compliment.*

Mame's Holiday Sweet Braid
  Oven—preheat to 350°
  Time—40 minutes
  Utensils—oiled bake sheet, cooling rack
  Ingredients—Basic sweet-bread recipe dough, 2-tablespoons flour for counter-top, 1-cup mixed glazed fruit, icing for top of baked loaf—1-cup powder sugar, 2-tablespoons soft butter, 1 ½-tablespoon milk, walnut halves, glazed cherries

  1—Knead glazed fruit into dough for two minutes.
  2—Divide dough into three pieces.
  3—Roll each piece back and forth to about 12" long.
  4—Place dough pieces on bake sheet and braid.
  5—Pinch ends together with few drops of water.
  6—Cover and allow dough to rise for 40 minutes.
  7—Bake 40 minutes—350°. Immediately remove bread to cooling rack.
  8—When cool, cover with icing and top with walnut halves and cherries.
  Or, make a holiday stollen—flatten dough and fold, not quite in half, and when baked decorate with icing, cherries and walnuts.
  Or, once braided bring the two ends together into a holiday wreath.
  Or, Bake in 8 ½" x 4 ½" pan and cover with Mame's sugar glaze:
  1-tablespoon hot water mixed with ¼-cup sugar.

♥ *During the 1920s and 1930s—Mame made holiday braid for her children—Mary and Ed. And, during the 1940s and 1950s Mame made holiday braid for her grandsons: Joe, Ed and Frank.*

Maureen's Peanut Butter Bread
    Oven—preheat to 350°
    Time—40 minutes
    Utensils—oiled bread pan, cooling rack
    Ingredients—Basic sweet-bread recipe dough, 2-tablespoons flour for counter top, 3/4-cup soft peanut butter-chunky or smooth

    1—Flatten dough with your fingers or rolling pin to 8" x 12".
    2—Cover dough with peanut butter.
    3—Firmly roll up dough, seal ends, and place in bread pan.
    4—Cover and allow dough to rise for 40 minutes.
    5—Make slash /// across the top.
    6—Bake 40 minutes—350°. Immediately remove bread from pan to cooling rack.
    Children—ages 3 to 93—enjoy this grand snack when camping or picnicking.

♥ *In the 1970s—We made peanut butter bread and with the next baking the suggestion was to make peanut butter and jelly bread: ¼ cup grape jelly and ½ cup peanut butter. Too much jelly makes dough awkward to roll and while baking, jelly spills out and burns. This bread was different and fun—a successful experiment.*

♥ *Many times children made ingredient suggestions and helped with the making. When the kitchen was filled with smoke, from spilled over ingredients, we knew to correct the ingredient amounts with the next bread baking.*

Mother's Sweet-Raisin-BreadMemory
    Oven—preheat to 350°
    Time—40 minutes
    Utensils—oiled bread pan 8 ½" x 4 ½", cooling rack
    Ingredients—Basic sweet-bread recipe dough, 2-tablespoons flour for counter top, 1-cup raisins, sugar glaze:1 tablespoon hot water with ¼-cup sugar.

    1—Flatten dough slightly with your fingers.
    2—Sprinkle raisins onto dough and knead into dough for about 2 minutes.
    3—Press flat again, roll up dough, tuck in ends and place into bread pan.
    4—Cover and allow dough to rise for 40 minutes.
    5—Make /// across the top. Bake 40 minutes—350°.
    6—Immediately remove to cooling rack and sprinkle on glaze.

Nuts and Golden Raisins
   Oven—preheat to 350°
   Time—40 minutes
   Utensil—oiled bake sheet or 8 ½" x 4 ½" bread pan, cooling rack
   Ingredients—Basic sweet-bread recipe dough, 2-tablespoons flour for counter
   top, 3-tablespoons soft butter, ½-cup chopped nuts—almonds, pecans of wal-
   nuts, 1-cup golden raisins

   1—Flatten dough with your fingers.
   2—Spread with butter, sprinkle on nuts and raisins.
   3—Firmly roll up dough and tuck in ends.
   4—Place dough onto baking sheet or bread pan.
   5—Cover and allow dough to rise for 40 minutes.
   6—Make slash /// across the top.
   7—Bake 40 minutes—350°. Immediately remove bread from pan to cooling
   rack.
   Golden raisins are sweeter than dark raisins.
   This bread has a memorable flavor and appearance.

Nutty Mincemeat
   Oven—preheat to 350°
   Time—40 minutes
   Utensil—oiled baking sheet, rolling pin, cooling rack
   Ingredients—Basic sweet-bread recipe dough, 2-tablespoons flour for counter
   top, ½-cup mincemeat, 1-cup ground walnuts

   1—With a rolling pin flatten dough to about 8" x 16".
   2—Mix mincemeat with ground walnuts.
   3—Place half mixture along 1/3 end of dough.
   4—Fold dough over mixture.
   5—Place remaining mixture for a layer look.
   6—Fold dough over and seal with a few drops of water.
   7—Cover and allow dough to rise for 40 minutes.
   8—Bake for 40 minutes—350°.
   9—Immediately remove bread from baking sheet to cooling rack.
   Cover nutty mincemeat with icing: 1-cup powder sugar, ½-teaspoon vanilla,
   1 ½-tablespoon milk. Mincemeat, you like it or you hate it.
   Mincemeat combines citrus, raisins and currants. And, in years past, this mixture included meat bits and alcohol to preserve.

♥ *Late 1970s—A young child visiting our family, questioned Maureen as to the ingredients in mincemeat. She answered, "Mincemeat pie is little bug pie." The child declined the mincemeat pie dessert.*

Prune Bread
　　Oven—preheat to 350°
　　Time—40 minutes
　　Utensils—oiled bread pan 8 ½" x 4 ½", cooling rack
　　Ingredients—Basic sweet-bread recipe dough, 2-tablespoons flour for counter top, 1 ½-cup chopped prunes

　　1—Slightly flatten dough with your fingers.
　　2—Sprinkle on chopped prunes.
　　3—Fold dough over prunes and knead for about 2 minutes to distribute prunes.
　　4—Again flatten dough, firmly roll, tuck in ends and place in bread pan.
　　5—Cover and allow 40 minutes to rise.
　　6—Make slash /// across the top.
　　7—Bake 40 minutes—350°.
　　8—Immediately remove bread from a pan to a cooling rack.
　　Do not bother to suggest this bread to a teenager; those with a mature palate will appreciate your efforts.

♥ *March '78—As he sorted through the frozen bread and read bread labels, Edward exclaimed with sarcasm, "Prune bread." He placed the bread back into the freezer and retrieved cinnamon bread.*

Basic sweet Five Loaf Favorites
After you have followed the one-loaf recipe a few times, you might find following the five-loaf recipes good fun. Good fun to prepare bread for everyday nutrition and good fun to freeze bread for holiday enjoyment. To further extend your good fun, check the suggestions for toppings and fillings in Chapter 6.

When following the five-loaf recipe, at step two you can add or substitute dry ingredients—grain, fruit, seeds etc. And at step three you can add or substitute liquid ingredients—honey, molasses etc. The breads freeze well, thaw nice and taste delicious.

Pans—before turning on the oven arrange and rearrange empty pans to find a fit. Five 8 ½" x 4 ½" pans, or five 8" x 4" pans, or ten 3" x 5" pans fit most home ovens, or one 13" x 9" with 9" cake pan and one 8 ½" x 4 ½" pan.

When I follow the five-loaf recipe, which is most of the time, I use either five bread pans or three 9" round pans and two 8 ½" x 4 ½" bread pans. Since only three round pans fit into the oven at once, and to slow down the rising, I hold the two bread pans in the refrigerator. When the bread in the three 9" pans is raised and placed into the oven, I remove the two bread pans from their holding place in the refrigerator. While the three rounds bake the dough in the two bread pans rises.

♥ *In the Early 1900s—Kneading flour for five-loaf recipe could be exhausting. But our Great grandmothers had sturdy hands, wrist and upper arms from washing, wringing and hanging clothes on the clothesline—women's work in the early 1900s.*

Raisin bread—For five loaves Raisin bread, at step two of the Basic sweet-bread recipe, add 8 cups raisins and continue with the recipe.

Raisin nut bread—For five loaves Raisin nut bread, at step two of the Basic sweet-bread recipe, add 6-cups raisins and 4-cups walnuts—chopped or whole, and continue with the recipe. Quite a bit of dough to hand knead. But when the bread is baked you will be rewarded with five magnificent loaves.

Holiday Loaf—For five loaves of Holiday bread, at step two of Basic recipe add 2-cups dark raisins, 2-cups golden raisins, 2-cups walnuts, 2-cups colorful mixed fruit peel and continue with the recipe. When baked, cover holiday bread with icing, whole nuts and glazed cherries.

With the next baking, add more or less fruit to your enjoyment.

♥ *On a day in 1977—Adelaide, my Medford Lakes neighbor, was making bread for guest, and wanted to follow the five-loaf recipe. But she found the dough too bulky to knead. Adelaide mixed the ingredients, and divided the dough into half for kneading. Although Adelaide enjoyed fresh baked bread, she said, "It tastes best toasted."*

♥*February 28ᵗʰ 1994*—*On the 26ᵗʰ, I followed the basic five-loaf recipe and used two portions for cinnamon buns. I refrigerated the remaining three portions for later use. Today, I removed the dough from the refrigerator, and allowed the dough to rise for 30 minutes before baking—a fast, no fuss sweet treat.*

Sweet Bread is made to Share—Double the Recipe

3

Basic Dark-Bread Recipe, Directions and Recipe Suggestions

This Basic dark bread has a naturally sweet whole-wheat flavor that is dense and delicious. The flour—100% whole wheat—makes hearty dough that does not have white dough elasticity, and will not bounce back if handled too much. For perfect presentation, when baking dark flour bread, use an 8" x 4" baking pan. This pan is slightly smaller than the bread pan used for Basic white and sweet bread. For additional reading look to Chapter 4—Mix, Knead, Bake and Serve.

Before starting to bake Basic dark bread, read through the directions, warm the immediate baking area and set out utensils and ingredients.

Basic Dark-Bread Recipe and Directions for One Loaf and Five Loaves

Baking Area
Area to knead dough (counter top/or table top) should be at least—24" x 34".
Area to Rest/Rise dough should be close to 80°. It is all right if area is not exactly 80°.
(Refer to Baking area, Oven, Time and Utensils in Chapter 4.)

Oven
Preheat oven to 350°

Time
Bake 40 minutes

˳ cups
.ring spoons
.ıxing spoon
Knife to level flour
Container to mix ingredients
Pot to heat liquid
Liquid thermometer
Room thermometer
Lightly oiled bread pan 8" x 4" or 8" round pan
Rolling pin—optional
Cooling rack

♦Because it packs the flour too densely, do not dip aluminum measuring cup into flour bag. Rather, place the cup on a plate or wax paper and spoon or pour from flour bag into the cup. Use a level measuring cup, and level flour with the straight side of a knife. Return the spilled over flour back into the flour container.

Basic Dark-Bread Recipe

Ingredients Basic dark bread—one loaf or five loaves
One Loaf
4-cups 100% whole-wheat flour
1-pkg dry yeast
2-teaspoons salt
1-tablespoon sugar
1-cup water
½-cup whole milk
2-tablespoons vegetable oil

Five Loaves
20-cups 100% whole-wheat flour
4-pkgs dry yeast
2-tablespoons salt
¼-cup sugar
4-cups water
2-cups whole milk
½-cup vegetable oil

Directions for Basic dark bread—one loaf or five loaves
1—Hold aside flour to use later. For the one-loaf recipe, hold aside ½ cup flour. For the five-loaf recipe, hold aside 1-cup flour. Otherwise, the directions are the same for one loaf or five loaves.

2—**Container**—With large spoon, mix the remaining flour, yeast, salt and sugar for about one minute.

3—**Pot**—On medium heat warm the water, milk and vegetable oil. When temperature reaches 130°, remove pot from heat. It is all right if liquid is not exactly 130°.

4—All at once pour the warm liquid into the container with dry ingredients, and mix with a large spoon. When the ingredients are too heavy to mix, gather together with your hands.

5—**Kneading dough**
    A—On a flat surface, sprinkle 1-tablespoon of the set aside flour.
    B—Turn mixture from container onto floured surface: rub flour from hands and from container.
    C—Gather dough together into one round.
    The dough might seem dry, but this will change with kneading.
    D—Flatten dough slightly and then fold the dough.
    E—Press dough firmly with the heel of you hands.
    F—Turn dough one quarter around.
    G—Repeat—flatten, fold, press firmly and turn.
    H—If dough sticks to the flat surface, add 1-tablespoon set aside flour as needed.
    I—Continue to flatten, fold, press and turn the dough for ten minutes.
    You have completed kneading.

6—**Resting dough**—Cover dough with a towel, and allow dough to rest for 15 minutes in an 80° baking area.

7—After 15 minutes, the dough will rise and be awkward to work with. Release the air by pressing down dough in a few places.

(If you follow the recipe for five loaves, now is the time to divide the dough into five loaves.
Five 8" x 4" pans fit into most kitchen ovens.)

(This is the Basic dark bread recipe dough called for on the following recipes—Cinnamon Whole Wheat, Coconut Whole Wheat, Currant Whole wheat etc.)

8—**Shaping dough**—Sprinkle 1-tablespoon flour onto flat surface. Fatten dough to about 8" x 12". Firmly roll up dough; tuck in ends, and place seam side down in 8" x 4" baking pan. There might be some flour left over, use it the next time you bake bread.

9—**Rising dough**—Cover dough with a light towel and let rise in 80° area for 40 minutes.

10—With a serrated knife cut a line 1/16 inch deep along the loaf. This encourages dough to bake even. (See Slash /// in Chapter 4.)

11—Bake in a preheated oven for 40 minutes. When baked, bread will be a crusty brown.

12—Immediately remove bread from pan to a cooling rack.

13—Congratulations you have made nutritious and delicious 100% whole-wheat bread.

One-Loaf Suggestions Basic Dark Dough

For a 100% whole wheat change, look to Basic dark one-loaf recipe suggestions—

Anise-Raisin Whole Wheat, Bulgur-Bits Whole Wheat, Carrot Nut Whole Wheat, Cinnamon Whole-Wheat, Coconut Date Whole Wheat, Currant Whole Wheat, Date Nut Whole Wheat, Flax Seed Whole Wheat, Golden Raisin Whole Wheat, Nutty Whole Wheat, Oats and Cinnamon Whole Wheat, Onion Whole Wheat, Orange Date/Nut Whole Wheat, Patty's Toasted Whole Wheat Germ, Pepper Whole Wheat, Pizza-Whole Wheat, Poppy Seed Whole Wheat, Whole Wheat Surprise

If you enjoy hearty Basic dark 100% whole wheat bread then experiment with other whole grains.

And, experiment with baking pans. Shape dough into a round and place on baking sheet. Roll and slice the dough and place onto 8" cake pan. When baked drizzle on a favorite topping. (Chapter 6, Tasty Toppings)

The recipes shown below call for additional ingredients in small amounts. As you bake a few loaves, adjust the amounts to suit your taste. For flavor change, use toasted wheat germ or corn meal in place of counter-top flour.

For sweeter bread, use additional brown sugar, honey or molasses.
For darker bread, use dark molasses for sweetener and add 2-teaspoons powder coffee or powder chocolate or both to the dry ingredients.

♥ *1980s–2000s—Because family and friends prefer Basic white and sweet bread, I seldom bake Basic dark bread. Yet when I do, I am thrilled with the sweet flavor and dense texture—and more thrilled when bulgur bits are added.*

♥ *1982—On a return trip from working in Munich, Germany, the airlines misplaced Ed's luggage. When Ed arrived home from the airport, he complained at length about the airlines mismanagement. Since clothing had never been Ed's priority, I could not understand his agitation.*
At 10:00 PM, the airline delivered his luggage. And with a great smile, Ed opened the luggage to reveal loaves of dark and seeded German bread—such a feast we had.

Anise seed-Raisin Whole Wheat Bread

Oven—preheat to 350°
Time—40 minutes
Utensils—oiled bread pan 8" x 4", cooling rack
Ingredients—Basic dark-bread recipe dough, 2-tablespoons whole-wheat flour or toasted wheat germ for counter top, 2-tablespoons anise seed, ½ cup raisins

1—Flatten dough slightly and sprinkle on anise seed and raisins.
2—Knead seeds and raisins into dough for about 2 minutes.
3—Firmly roll up dough and shape for bread pan.
4—Place in pan, cover and allow 40 minutes to rise.
5—Bake 40 minutes—350°.
6—Immediately remove from oven and place on cooling rack.
Drizzle on icing and sprinkle with anise seed.
This bread combines fiber with flavor.

Bulgur bits-Whole Wheat

Oven—preheat to 350°
Time—40 minutes
Utensil—oiled 8" x 4" bread pan, cooling rack
Ingredients—Basic dark-bread recipe dough, 2-tablespoons whole-wheat flour for counter top, ½-cup bulgur

1—Flatten dough slightly and sprinkle on bulgur.
2—Knead into dough for about 2 minutes.
3—Firmly roll up dough, and shape for bread pan.
4—Place in pan, cover and allow 40 minutes to rise.
5—Make /// slash across the top.
6—Bake 40 minutes—350°.
7—Immediately remove bread from pan to cooling rack.
The crisp bulgur bits give this bread additional texture, a nice bite and exceptional flavor. And when toasted the warmth and the crisp with a bit of cheese makes for a grand lunch.

Carrot-Nut Whole Wheat
  Oven—preheat to 350°
  Time—40 minutes
  Utensil—oiled baking sheet, cooling rack
  Ingredients—Basic dark-bread recipe dough, 2-tablespoons whole-wheat flour
  for counter top, ½-cup shredded carrot, ½-cup chopped walnuts

  1—Flatten dough slightly and sprinkle on carrot and walnuts.
  2—Knead for about 2 minutes and shape into a round.
  3—Place on baking sheet, cover and allow dough to rise for 40 minutes.
  4—Make slash /// across the top.
  5—Bake 40 minutes—350°.
  6—Immediately remove bread from pan to cooling rack.
  A tasty afternoon snack when this whole-wheat bread is sandwiched with
  cream cheese.

♥ *High nutrition breads, made with whole grains, are feel-good breads: you feel good making bread, eating bread and receiving compliments.*

Cinnamon whole wheat
  Oven—preheat to 350°
  Time—40 minutes
  Utensils—oiled 8" x 4" bread pan, cooling rack
  Ingredients—Basic dark-bread recipe dough, 2-tablespoons whole-wheat flour
  or toasted wheat germ for counter top, 3-tablespoons soft butter, 3-table-
  spoons granulated sugar, 1-tablespoon cinnamon,

  1—Flatten dough with your fingers to about 8" x 12".
  2—Spread butter onto dough.
  3—Mix cinnamon and sugar and sprinkle onto dough.
  4—Roll dough, to fit pan, and seal ends together.
  5—Place in pan, cover and allow dough to rise for 40 minutes.
  6—Bake 40 minutes—350°.
  7—Immediately remove bread from pan to cooling rack.
  This sweet whole wheat bread requires no additional topping.

Coconut Date Whole Wheat

Oven—preheat to 350°
Time—40 minutes
Utensil—oiled baking sheet, cooling rack
Ingredients—Basic dark-bread recipe dough, 2-tablespoons whole-wheat flour for counter top, ½-cup chopped dates, ½-cup coconut

1—Flatten dough slightly and sprinkle on dates and coconut.
2—Knead ingredients into dough for about 2 minutes.
3—Firmly roll up dough, and place on baking sheet.
4—Place in pan, cover and allow 40 minutes to rise.
5—Make /// slash across the top.
6—Bake 40 minutes—350°.
7—Immediately remove bread from pan to cooling rack.
This is dark and flavorful bread that combines sweet coconut crunch with the moist date

Currant Nut Whole Wheat

Oven—preheat to 350°
Time—40 minutes
Utensils—oiled 8 ½" x 4 ½" bread pan, cooling rack
Ingredients—Basic dark-bread recipe dough, 2-tablespoons dark flour for counter top, 1-cup currants

1—Flatten dough slightly with your fingers.
2—Sprinkle on currants, and knead dough for about 2 minutes.
3—Flatten dough, roll and shape for bread pan.
4—Place in bread pan, cover and allow dough to rise for 40 minutes.
5—Make slash /// across the top.
6—Bake 40 minutes—350°.
7—Immediately remove bread from pan to cooling rack.
Serve with chunky applesauce and aged sharp cheese.

Date nut Whole Wheat
Oven—preheat to 350°
Time—40 minutes
Utensil—oiled 8" x 4" bread pan, cooling rack
Ingredients—Basic dark-bread recipe dough, 2-tablespoons whole-wheat flour for counter top, ½-cup date pieces, ½-cup chopped walnuts

1—Flatten dough slightly, and sprinkle on date and walnut pieces.
2—Knead about 2 minutes.
3—Firmly roll up dough, tuck in ends, and place seam side down in bread pan.
4—Cover and allow 40 minutes to rise.
5—Make /// slash across the top.
6—Bake 40 minutes—350°.
7—Immediately remove bread from pan to a cooling rack.
This bread is moist for brown bagging, and a lunchtime treat when lathered with honey.

♥ *Ed's first question, when bread aroma sends him to the kitchen, "Did you make my favorite date-nut bread?"*

Flax Seed Whole Wheat
Oven—preheat to 350°
Time—40 minutes
Utensil—oiled 8" x 4" bread pan or bake sheet, cooling rack
Ingredients—Basic dark-bread recipe dough, 2-tablespoons whole-wheat flour for counter top, ½-cup flax seeds

1—Flatten dough slightly and sprinkle on flax seeds.
2—Knead into dough for about 2 minutes.
3—Firmly roll up dough, tuck in ends, and place seam side down in baking pan.
4—Cover and allow 40 minutes to rise. Make /// slash across the top.
5—Bake 40 minutes—350°.
6—Immediately remove bread from pan to a cooling rack.
Flax seeds seem to multiply; for there are as many speckled throughout the bread as there are on counter and floor.

♥*Mid 1980s—A German friend, Herbert, said of the French, "They only make white bread."*
Another German man said that when he had a contract to work in France he would not eat French bread. He traveled to France weekly with two suitcases: one filled with round loaves of dark, dense German whole wheat bread.

Golden Raisin Whole Wheat

Oven—preheat to 350°
Time—40 minutes
Utensil—oiled baking sheet, cooling rack
Ingredients—Basic dark-bread recipe dough, 2-tablespoons wheat flour for counter top, 1-cup golden raisins

1—Flatten dough slightly, and sprinkle on raisins.
2—Knead about 2 minutes and flatten into a round.
3—Place dough onto baking sheet, cover and allow 40 minutes to rise.
4—Make slash /// across the top.
5—Bake 40 minutes—350°.
6—Immediately remove bread from pan to a cooling rack.
Try a slice with cinnamon and sugar, and a second slice with butter and honey.

Nutty Whole Wheat

Oven—preheat to 350°
Time—40 minutes
Utensil—oiled 8" x 4" bread pan, cooling rack
Ingredients—Basic dark-bread recipe dough, 2-tablespoons whole-wheat flour for counter top, ½-cup chopped nuts—your choice

1—Flatten dough slightly.
2—Sprinkle on nuts and knead into dough for about 2 minutes.
3—Flatten dough to 8" x 12", shape into loaf and place seam side down in baking pan.
4—Cover and allow 40 minutes to rise.
5—Make /// slash across the top.
6—Bake 40 minutes—350°.
7—Immediately remove bread from pan to a cooling rack.
This is a nutritious snack when toasted and topped with apple butter.

Oats and Cinnamon Whole Wheat

Oven—preheat to 350°
Time—40 minutes
Utensils—oiled bread pan 8" x 4", or bake sheet, cooling rack
Ingredients—Basic dark-bread recipe dough, 2-tablespoons oats for counter top, 3 tablespoons soft butter, ¼-cup quick-cooking oats, 1-tablespoon cinnamon, ¼-cup sugar

1—Flatten dough slightly, and brush with butter.
2—Mix oats, cinnamon/sugar and sprinkle onto dough.
3—Firmly roll up dough and shape into a loaf.
4—Place in bake pan, cover and allow dough to rise for 40 minutes.
5—Bake 40 minutes—350°.
6—Immediately remove bread from pan to cooling rack.
This is breakfast oatmeal at its best with whole-wheat nutrition, cinnamon flavor and sweet-goodness—
Icing: 1-cup powder sugar, ½ teaspoon vanilla, and 1 ½ tablespoon milk.

Onion Whole Wheat

Oven—preheat to 350°
Time—40 minutes
Utensil—oiled baking sheet, cooling rack
Ingredients—Basic dark-bread recipe dough, 2-tablespoons toasted wheat germ for counter top, 3 tablespoons dry onions, 2-tablespoons corn meal
For dry onions, separate the dry onions from the powder—salt/spice—in onion soup mix.

1—Flatten dough slightly, and sprinkle onions onto dough.
2—Knead for about 2 minutes and flatten into a round.
3—Sprinkle corn meal on oiled baking sheet and place dough atop.
4—Cover and allow 40 minutes to rise.
5—Make /// slash across the top. Bake 40 minutes—350°.
6—Immediately remove bread from pan to a cooling rack.
While the bread is baking the home has a delicious onion aroma.

Orange Date-Nut Whole Wheat

Oven—preheat to 350°
Time—40 minutes
Utensils—oiled bread pan 8" x 4", cooling rack
Ingredients—Basic dark-bread recipe dough, 2-tablespoons whole-wheat flour for counter top, ½-cup chopped dates, ½-cup chopped nuts, 2-tablespoon grated orange peel

1—Flatten dough slightly, and sprinkle on ingredients.
2—Knead ingredients into dough for about 2 minutes.
3—Shape into a loaf, tuck in ends and place seam side down in pan.
4—Cover and allow dough to rise for 40 minutes.
5—Make slash /// across the top.
6—Bake 40 minutes—350°.
7—Immediately remove bread from pan to a cooling rack.
When cool, cover with orange icing: 1-cup powder sugar, 2-tablespoons orange juice, and 1-tablespoon grated orange peel

Patty's Wheat-Germ Nutrition

Oven—preheat to 350°
Time—40 minutes
Utensil—oiled bread pan 8" x 4" or bake sheet, cooling rack
Ingredients—Basic dark-bread recipe dough, ½-cup toasted wheat germ

1—Sprinkle ¼ toasted wheat germ onto counter, and flattened dough slightly on top of wheat germ.
2—Sprinkle ¼-cup toasted wheat germ onto flattened dough, and knead for 2 minutes.
3—Roll and shape into a loaf. The outer dough will have wheat germ bits.
4—Tuck in ends, place in pan or on baking sheet, cover and allow 40 minutes to rise.
5—Make /// slash across the top.
6—Bake 40 minutes—350°.
7—Immediately remove bread from pan to a cooling rack.
This high fiber wheat germ bread has a speckled look and good flavor.

♥*Mid 1900s—My daughter-in-law Patty is nutrition conscious. Her comments, about high nutrition wheat-germ bread pleased the baker.*

Pepper Whole Wheat
  Oven—preheat to 350°
  Time—40 minutes
  Utensil—oiled 8" x 4" bread pan, sharp knife, cooling rack
  Ingredients—Basic dark-bread recipe dough, 2-tablespoons whole-wheat flour or toasted wheat germ for counter top, ½-cup red pepper (not cooked), ½-teaspoon red pepper flakes

  1—Flatten dough slightly and sprinkle on the pepper pieces and flakes.
  2—Knead into the dough for one minute.
  3—Flatten dough to 8" x 12", shape for loaf and place seam side down on bread pan.
  4—Cover and allow dough to rise for 40 minutes.
  (When using hot pepper, do not rub your eyes.
  And wash your hands and work area to remove the hot pepper.)
  5—Make /// slash across the top.
  6—Bake 40 minutes—350°.
  7—Immediately remove bread from pan to a cooling rack.
  With the next baking, add red pepper flakes according to taste tolerance.

Pizza Whole Wheat
  Oven—preheat to 350°
  Time—40 minutes
  Utensils—oiled pizza pan or baking sheet, cheese grater, spoon, sharp knife
  Ingredients—Basic dark-bread recipe dough, 2-tablespoons wheat flour for counter top, 1 ½-cups tomato sauce, 8 oz-mozzarella cheese, 1-teaspoon Italian spice, 2-tablespoon olive oil,

  1—Flatten dough enough to cover an oiled pizza pan or baking sheet.
  2—Spread sauce, sprinkle on cheese, spice and olive oil.
  3—Allow dough to rise for 40 minutes.
  4—Bake 40 minutes 350°. Immediately remove bread from pan to a cooling rack.
  The mature pallet will enjoy whole-wheat vegetable pizza with the works: broccoli, spinach, peppers, onions, tomatoes, cheese and spice.

♥ *September 16th 1986—Maureen made a comment about whole-wheat pizza, "Nice brown bread, but no excitement to the taste buds." In fact, you would think the baker served poison pizza.*

Poppy-Seed Walnut Whole Wheat

Oven—preheat to 350°

Time—40 minutes

Utensils—oiled bread pan 8" x 4", cooling rack

Ingredients—Basic dark bread recipe dough, 2-tablespoons flour for counter top, ¼-cup poppy seeds, ½-cup chopped walnuts

1—Flatten dough with your fingers.

2—Sprinkle with poppy seeds and walnuts, and knead for about 2 minutes.

3—Firmly roll up dough, tuck in ends and place in bread pan.

4—Cover and allow dough to rise for 40 minutes.

5—Make slash /// across the top.

6—Bake 40 minutes—350°.

7—Immediately remove bread from pan to a cooling rack.

Before you decide against this bread, eat two slices.

♥ *1970s—While the children look on in disdain, Ed finds poppy seed whole-wheat bread flavorful.*

Whole Wheat Surprise
Oven—preheat to 350°
Time—40 minutes
Utensil—oiled bread pan 8" x 4", cooling rack
Ingredients—Basic dark-bread recipe dough, 2-tablespoons whole-wheat flour
or wheat germ for counter top, ¼-cup chopped dates, ¼-cup chopped pecans,
¼-cup shredded coconut

1—Flatten dough to about 8" x 12" and sprinkle on dates, nuts and coconut.
2—Knead for about 2 minutes and shape for loaf. Place dough seam side
down in baking pan.
3—Cover and allow 40 minutes to rise.
4—Make /// slash across the top.
5—Bake 40 minutes—350°.
6—Immediately remove bread from pan to a cooling rack.
This crunchy high-fiber bread makes a flavorful midnight snack.

♥ *Saturday, December 5ᵗʰ 1992—We attended the morning ceremony for the
Army and Navy game with my work friend Angelica and Ed's fly fishing friend Bob.
And for lunch we enjoyed hearty wheat-bread sandwiches, which we needed to fortify
ourselves throughout the cold windy afternoon game. Ed had been in the Army during
the Korean Conflict and Bob served in the Vietnam War. Go Army!*

Home Baked Bread is Nutrition for Vegetarian and Macrobiotic Diets.

4

Mix, Knead, Bake and Serve

Use this chapter to check out—Baking Area, Buying Ingredients, Bread Machine, Dough Hook, Freezing Bread, Freezing Dough, Heating Liquid, Kneading Dough, Labeling, Measuring, Microwave Oven, Mixing Dry Ingredients, Mixing Liquid Ingredients, Oven, Pans, Perfection, Planning, Problems, Purchasing Bread, Recipe Reading, Refrigerator, Resting Dough, Rising Dough, Shaping Dough, Slash ///, Storage, Substitute Ingredients, Temperature, Time Necessary, Utensils and Yeast Guessing Removed.

When I read bread recipes that were written years ago, I recognize what bakers endured: cold rooms, wood fires and homemade yeast. Remarkable. Now bread makers have central heat, reliable ovens and dated yeast packets. Unfortunately, the new baker has heard many 'old wives tales' about yeast baking, and hesitates to try yeast baking. But with room, liquid and oven thermometers the guessing has been removed. See thermometers in this chapter.

When following the Basic bread recipes, 'about', 'relax' and 'not exactly' are words to remember. Knead the dough about 10 minutes. Let the dough rest about 15 minutes. Let the dough rise in about an 80° area for about 40 minutes. Relax. The time does not have to be exactly on the minute.

♥ *In years past, the time for bread rising lasted three hours, even overnight. The baker knew to depress dough with a finger, and if the depression stayed, then dough could be placed in bread baking pans. The dough had raised all it was going to raise. If the depression marks disappeared, then dough needed longer to rise. It worked. After the successful first rising time, dough was formed into loaves and again allowed to rise until well over the rim of the baking pan.*

1960s—For years, I made two loaves in five hours following the finger testing—guessing—method. Now, I make five loaves in two hours following the Basic bread recipe in this book—no guessing.

Baking Area
On most days (winter heater/summer air conditioner) kitchens register around seventy degrees. If your baking area is too cool, set dough close to the stove's heat-units, or in a pan over hot water. It is all right if the immediate area is not continuously 80°. For a gas stove, turn the units on high until the immediate area is 80°, and then turn off the units. As the area cools, again turn on units and watch closely until the area is again 80°. Some folks turn the oven on low and leave the door ajar. Supervise the kitchen area while units are on. And remember to adjust the oven heat for baking.

I have lived in homes that have had large or small kitchens, and know that it does not matter if you have small/medium/large kitchen. It matters that you have a space—counter, kitchen table or card table—where you control the warmth. That is, where you can keep the kneading and rising area around 80°.

♥ *1970s—In Medford Lakes, Maureen and Anna and their young friends used the family room, side porch or garage, which never held a car, for theatre, board games, homework etc. The areas were close to the baking area, and as a baker I could be available yet be occupied.*

♥ *1960s—My Levit-built Willingboro home is remembered for its great wrap-around kitchen counter space. 1990s—My present home in Medford has a kneading area that measures 2' x 3'. Either wrap around or 2' x 3, I control the heat in the baking area by keeping two stove units on low.*

Buying Bread-Making Ingredients
When buying ingredients, be mindful of the 'Best if purchased by date'.
The Basic white, sweet, dark bread ingredients—flour, vegetable oil, yeast, milk, salt, sugar, eggs and even water can be purchased from supermarkets and most convenience stores.
Because all-purpose flour and vegetable oil are familiar ingredients and readily available at the supermarket, they are recommended in the Basic white, sweet and dark recipes. (See Chapter 5, Ingredients that Change Taste and Texture.)

Flour—For Basic white and sweet bread, start with all-purpose flour and become familiar with how the ingredients interact with each other.

Flour—For Basic dark bread purchase 100% whole-wheat flour.

Salt—Use either iodized or not.

Sugar—A first time baker should use granulated sugar.

Yeast—The yeast packets show an expiration date.

Fat—Use vegetable oil or olive oil that is sold for cake and bread baking.

Liquid—Use water and/or whole milk.

Eggs—A medium or large egg.

♥ *1970s—At a health-food store, I purchased whole-wheat flour. After the time spent mixing, kneading etc., the newly baked bread tasted stale. The flour had been on the shelf too long, and, in fact, when purchasing the flour, I thought the flour bag seemed a bit dusty.*

Bread Machine

Since the bread machine kneads the bread ingredients, using a bread machine is tempting. And while bread is baking there is wonderful aroma and when baked, the bread taste fine. But the machine holds only enough dough for two loaves. There is no opportunity to make extra loaves for freezing or gift giving. And the machine is awkward to bring out of storage. Hand kneading, once learned, is never awkward. Because the machine is sensitive to ingredient weight etc., when using a bread machine, it is best to follow the recipes included with the machine.

Dough Hook

For hands-off bread baking, try a dough hook. A dough hook gives homemade excellence with store-bought texture. Follow the Basic white, sweet or dark bread recipe for one loaf. But, as with the bread machine, there is little extra for family and friends.

Shown here are the Basic white-bread recipe ingredients, but the Basic sweet and dark ingredients could also be used.

Dough-hook bread making directions
Oven: preheat to 350°
Time: 40 minutes
Utensils: dough hook, mixer, oiled bread pan 8 ½" x 4 ½", cooling rack
Ingredients: 4-cups flour, 1-pkg yeast, 1-tablespoon sugar, 2 teaspoon salt, 1-cup water, ½-cup milk, 2-tablespoons oil

Hold aside ½-cup flour.
1—Place dry ingredients—3½-cups flour, yeast, sugar, salt in the mixing bowl.
2—Blend on low for about one minute.
3—All at once add 130° liquids—water, milk, oil and continue to blend for three minutes.
4—Mix for two more minutes, while adding some of the remaining flour—if necessary.
5—Mix until dough does not feel too sticky. Remove the dough hook.
6—Cover dough with a towel, and allow dough to rest in the bowl for 15 minutes.
7—Press down the air from the raised dough, and remove dough to a floured surface.
8—Flatten and shape into a loaf and place into lightly oiled bread pan.
9—Cover and allow dough to rise for 40 minutes.
10—Bake 40 minutes at 350°.
11—Immediately remove to cooling rack.
The dough hook encourages the baker to add ingredients shown in Chapter 5.

♥ *September 10th, 1991—We purchased a new mixer with a dough hook. No more hand kneading. Great fun. The bread texture and color is acceptable and the bread has great flavor. But, there is always a 'but', the mixing-bowl size allows only enough ingredients for two loaves—no extra bread for family, friends and freezer.*

♥ *June 2000—I was diagnosed with breast cancer. Although I had not used the dough hook in years, I liked the convenience, and stayed with dough-hook kneading through my time on chemotherapy. A temporary arrangement*

Freezing Bread
To freeze bread, completely cool the just-baked bread, then wrap and seal tightly for the freezer. Do not leave open space—air—around the loaf. Freeze baked bread for up to six months. If you do not have a good freezer, after a month, the

bread will start to get freezer burn—dry white-burn as opposed to a crisp black-burn. Experiment with your freezer: freeze a loaf and check periodically.

♦ Slice bread before freezing, and use a slice as needed without thawing the whole loaf. Defrost a slice in the toaster.

♦ When bread-slices are frozen in individual sandwich bags, the slices are thawed by lunchtime and fresh tasting.

Thawing Bread

It is best to thaw frozen bread at room temperature for four hours, and then heat in the oven for a few minutes at 250°. (See Microwave oven)

Freezing Dough

To freeze bread dough, first allow kneaded dough to rest for the recommended 15 minutes. Then immediately—without raising—wrap tightly with freezer wrap and freeze. Or, shape dough into loaves, tightly wrap and freeze. If not tightly sealed, dough will expand and push open the wrapping. The exposed dough will get freezer burn, which leaves dough tasteless. Should this happen, cut away the freezer burned part before baking. Otherwise the freezer burn area will bake as a lump in your tasty bread.

♦ Freeze dough for days, weeks or months.

♦ Do not use aluminum foil to freezer-wrap dough. When dough thaws, aluminum foil adheres to the thawing dough. What a mess.

Thawing Dough

There are four ways to thaw frozen dough—24 hours in the refrigerator; 3–4 hours at 70° room temperature; a few minutes in oven (see oven); a few seconds in microwave (see microwave). Because the other three methods require too much attention (for me), the best method is 24 hours in the refrigerator.

♥ *March 1st 1995—Months ago, I placed dough on the shelf in the freezer door. When dough is placed in the freezer, dough continues to expand until the cold stops the growth. In this case, dough expanded enough to wedge itself into the shelf. I thought, if I waited until the moisture evaporated and freezer burn set in then the dough would shrink back, and I would be able to remove dough from the freezer. Not so. I had to defrost the whole freezer to soften the dough enough to remove it. The lesson learned is to wrap the dough tightly before placing onto the freezer shelf—not the door.*

HeatingLiquids
The Basic recipes call for liquids: water, milk and oil. Combine liquids, and heat until thermometer reaches 130°. 'The watched pot never boils,' but turn your back and water, milk and oil are boiling over. To avoid this, heat only the water to 160° then add cold milk and oil. Or heat the liquid in the microwave oven for 1½-minutes.

♦ If the watched pot does boil, reduce heat of liquid by placing the hot pot in a sink filled with cold water for minute or two. The liquid ingredients will cool down immediately.

♦ I have been known to cool hot liquid by adding a few ice cubes.

Kneading Dough
When preparing dough, have the area close to 80°. If you worry that the baking area is not warm enough, read up on Baking area and Temperature in this chapter.

Knead dough to distribute gas formed by water, yeast and flour. Kneading dough allows you to fold and press air into dough, and kneading helps distributes the yeast. Because machines knead air into dough, store-bought bread has a smooth texture. In comparison, hand kneaded, homemade bread has slightly coarse texture, which bread bakers enjoy.

Kneading Dough for ten minutes
When kneading dough, consider dough as having a top—the part away from you, and a bottom—the part close to you. Fold top toward bottom. Press dough firmly with the heel of your hands. Give the flattened dough a turn. Repeat: fold, press firmly and turn for 10 minutes. Have your feet firmly placed on the floor, and use the full strength of your upper body. Use one hand to fold dough, two hands to firmly press, and one hand to turn. Do what is comfortable for you: right hand, left hand or both hands.

As with resting and raising dough, bakers follow different kneading methods (See You Decide—Resting, Raising). For me, the two-hand method is most comfortable. But those who have great upper body strength prefer the one-hand method. I find that the men in the bread baking class whip that dough around the counter with one hand.

As you knead the dough it will feel a bit moist/sticky to the touch. Since the dough should not be dry, this is perfectly acceptable. But if the dough sticks to the counter then use some of the set aside flour. After 10 minutes, cover the dough and allow to rest.

♥**Early 1900s**—When kneading dough, Ed's grandmother Mame did not like sticky flour on her hands. To avoid this, she lightly rubbed lard onto her hands and then kneaded the dough.

♥ *2000s—When kneading dough at the bread baking class, I use disposable latex gloves. Although they are cumbersome to me, the students do not seem to find the gloves a bother.*

Kneading Fruit/NutsInto Dough
Fruit and nuts can be added at step two in the Basic recipe.
Or fruit and nuts can be kneaded into the dough from the Basic recipe.
To knead fruit and/or nuts into dough, first flatten the dough slightly with your fingers. Next distribute fruit/nuts evenly over dough—this shortens the kneading time—then fold dough and knead for 2-minutes. Shape into a loaf and set to rise for 40 minutes.

♥ *Elaine Tait, food editor for the "Philadelphia Inquirer" and now retired, stated in an article that when kneading dough the counter should appear to have a white dusting of snow.*
When my young grandchildren children help with bread baking, snow dust is on child, counter and floor, and snow prints are throughout the house.

Labeling
When freezing dough or bread, it is best to label the package with the bread name, date and ingredient information. Nothing disappoints more than to set ones taste buds on sweet bread and thaw savory bread.

When sharing baked bread with family and friends they might wish to know what your bread loaf contains. Label ingredients according to inclusion: flour, water, milk, oil, eggs, sugar, salt and yeast. With digestive problems and allergies, folks are comfortable knowing the ingredients—particularly eggs and nuts.

♥ *November 23ʳᵈ 2003—When giving bread to a friend or donating bread for a bazaar, I show the ingredients with an e-Mail address on the label.*
After I followed the five-loaf raisin bread recipe for the Haddon Heights Bazaar, I received this reply, "We have just finished enjoying the best ever raisin bread you donated to the bazaar. If you bake it often, we would like to be among your customers…" WGS

Measuring
When measuring ingredients for the Basic bread recipe, the liquid, fat, and sweetener along with the atmosphere in your kitchen makes a difference in the flour amount necessary. The type of flour: all-purpose white or 100% whole wheat also makes a difference. By suggesting that set-aside flour be used as needed, the Basic recipe allows for this difference. The set-aside flour might all be used, then again there might be flour left over for the next baking.

Measure
16-oz = 1 pt
2-cups = 1 pt
4-cups = 1 qt
A cupful—a full measuring cup leveled off with straight side of a knife.
1-cup = 8 oz
4-tablespoons = ¼-cup
3-teaspoon = 1-tablespoons
Pinch—amount that can be held between thumb and index finger

♥ *Learning fractions become meaningful to small children when they recognize the numerator/denominator—¼/½ cup—necessary to measure sweetbread toppings.*

Miscellaneous Measures
½ lb butter = 1-cup = 2-sticks
Measure butter by packing solid butter into a cup and leveling.
Scant cup—a bit less than a cup
4-oz flour = 1-cup
1-lb flour = 4-cups
2-lbs flour = 8 cups
3-lbs flour = 12-cups
4-lbs flour = 16 cups
5-lbs flour = 20-cups
4-oz wheat germ = 1-cup
5-oz corn meal = 1-cup
1-medium egg = ¼-cup
1-qt milk = 4-cups
6-oz raisins = 1-cup
6-oz dates = 1-cup
7-oz sugar = 1-cup
¼-lb walnuts = 1-cup
1-pkg active dry yeast = 1-pkg rapid rise
1-pkg yeast = 1 cake fresh yeast
1-pkg yeast = 2 ¼-teaspoon
1,000-mg salt = 1 g

♥ *Sayings used when weighing situations in life-*
Know which side your bread is buttered (know whom you can depend on).
He knows who butters his bread (who is paying his bill).
Butter your own bread (depend on yourself).
Don't spend too much time on the crumb crushers in life (think big).
He has a large breadbasket (stomach).
Let us break bread together (have dinner).
How much bread (money)?
Send a bread and butter note (thank you note).
Stand in a bread line (food line).

♥ *Early 2000s—When my volunteer group, at Virtua Memorial Hospital, meets for potluck lunch, it is a given that I will make bread.*

Microwave Oven

Frozen dough can be brought to room temperature in the microwave oven, and baked bread can be warmed in the microwave oven. But, do not use the microwave oven to bake bread. The microwave oven cooks bread from the inside out. Thus a loaf can feel baked to touch, over cooked inside and the flavor unpleasant.

Microwave oven rising dough

The microwave oven requires too much attention to rise, warm or thaw dough. If you wish to experiment keep in mind that dough has little moisture, and moisture is necessary for microwave oven heating. Place a small dish filled with water in the microwave oven when rising, warming or thawing dough.

Microwave Oven Thawing Dough

If you choose to thaw frozen dough in the microwave oven, place frozen dough on shelf with a small container of water. Cover dough with paper towel. After a few seconds in the microwave oven, the dough texture is cold and granular to touch. Knead dough for two minutes. This distributes the inner warm into still cold outer dough.

Microwave Oven Warming Dough

If you choose to warm dough (that has been in the refrigerator) in the microwave oven, cover dough with paper towel and place in the microwave oven with a small container of water. After a few seconds, remove from microwave oven and knead dough (add fruit/nuts) on a floured surface, for two minutes and shape.

Microwave Oven Thawing Bread

When thawing baked bread in the microwave oven use caution. In one minute, a full loaf will defrost enough for slicing. A few **seconds** too long and bread will be past eating. Watch closely. For a few frozen bread slices use the toaster on low.

♥ *Mid 1980s—After I was secure in bread baking knowledge, I thought to help others to bake bread at home. An advertisement placed in the local newspaper brought a few telephone calls. One retired man told me that he had been baking bread for years, but wanted bread-baking lessons. My question, "Does your family and friends enjoy the bread that you bake." He replied, "Yes, they request that I make bread for them all the time." My reply, "You do not need to waste time learning how to bake bread."*

Mixing Dry Ingredients
In baking bread, as opposed to baking cakes, ingredients do not have to be exact. If you measure a bit too much flour then you need a bit more liquid, too much liquid then bit more flour etc.

Since yeast likes cozy, have dry ingredients at room temperature. When mixing dry ingredients, thoroughly blend the ingredients then add liquid ingredients.

Although the yeast is the least amount, yeast controls the results. With a large spoon blend the dry ingredients: flour, sugar, salt and yeast for about one minute. (Give about sixty spoon-turns through dry ingredients.) The liquid, at 130°, is far too hot to pour directly onto yeast. But after yeast has thoroughly mixed through the other dry ingredients, the hot liquid blends the ingredients.

Adding Dry ingredients to Dough
When adding dry ingredients: fruit, nuts etc to dough, which is already kneaded there are a few steps to follow. First flatten the dough and cover the dough with melted butter—otherwise when the dough is baked the bread will separate/ unravel when sliced. Then sprinkle on the dry ingredients. Finally, firmly roll and slice the dough for baking.
But when kneading additional dry ingredients into dough that will be baked as a loaf and not rolled and sliced, the butter is not necessary.

Mixing Liquid Ingredients
When mixing liquid, combined the liquid ingredients: water, milk, and oil and heat until 130°. All at once pour 130° liquids into the container with the blended dry ingredients and mix together with a large spoon. Kneading further distributes the ingredients, and the dough will be smooth and easy to work with. A first time baker might think this a pasty mess. This pasty mess will soon blend into dough and bake into delicious bread.

Mixing Eggs
When measuring eggs the rule is to add hot to cold (heated milk, water, oil to cold eggs) and not cold to hot (cold eggs to hot water, milk, oil). If cold eggs are added to hot liquid, eggs solidify (scramble) rather then blend. Solid eggs pieces will then be in the dough.
There are two methods for mixing eggs. Use the first method when adding one egg.

First method for mixing eggs—Worry free
A—Mix heated water, milk and oil with dry ingredients: flour, sugar, salt and yeast.
B—Add fork beaten egg.
C—Blend in the egg. (See Kneading)

Use the second method if eggs are cold from the refrigerator and you are following the five-loaf recipe.
Second method for mixing eggs—Use caution
A—Gradually introduce some 130° liquids into bowl with cold fork-blended eggs.
B—Combine this mixture with all 130° liquids.
C—Retest liquid for 130°.
D—Immediately blend combined 130° liquids with dry ingredients.

Mixing five loaf ingredients'
When following the five-loaf recipe, I use a 3 ½-qt pot to heat the liquid and a 16-qt container for mixing together dry and liquid ingredients.

♥ *In the early 1900's—My mother watched her mother Anna take flour by the handful, add other dry ingredients, then make a well in the dry ingredients and pour in the liquid ingredients.*

♥ *Mid 1960s—My mother said, "Mom never used a recipe, measuring cups or spoons. She made good-tasting bread with a handful of this, and a pinch of that. She used the surface of the kitchen table to mix ingredients and knead dough. The kneaded dough was covered with a cloth, and set to rise by the coal fire."*

♥ *1960s—Although my mother never baked bread, when I started to bake bread, my mother shared her childhood-bread memories with me. But unlike my grandmother Anna, I cannot mix ingredients on the flat surface—kitchen table or counter top. It seems impossible for me to make a well in flour and pour in liquid ingredients without making a mess. I use a container to mix liquid and dry ingredients. The dough is kneaded on the counter top, and for warmth the kneaded dough is set close to stove units that are turned to low.*

♥ *2000s—When my young granddaughters help me to blend bread-baking ingredients, I place the large pot on the floor for them to observe. They add and mix the dry ingredients. I heat and add the liquid ingredients. After I knead the dough, they have fun creating shapes and adding cinnamon, raisins, butter etc.*

Oven

Become acquainted with your oven—too hot, too cold or just right. To double check oven interior, purchase an oven gauge. Because hot air circulates evenly, when baking bread, use the middle shelf.

Bread can be baked for a shorter time at a higher temperature. And bread can be baked for a longer time at a lower temperature. The Basic recipes call for baking bread 40 minutes at 350°.

It takes 7 to 10 minutes for an oven to reach 350°. Each time the oven door is open, hot air escapes; this can reduce interior oven heat by as much as 50°. Once placed into the oven, dough will continue to rise until the intense heat kills the yeast cells.

If temperature is too high, yeast cells outside the loaf are killed too fast and a tough crust builds. When this happens, the interior dough cannot rise, resulting in a low, dense, soggy dough with a tough crust.

If oven temperature is too low, yeast cells continue to expand until the loaf falls, resulting in flat, dry, chewy, dough with a bad taste.

♦ A first-time baker should check the loaf during the last ten minutes. An oven light resolves questions.

♦ If the bread browns too fast, cover with aluminum foil and continue to bake (check oven gage).

♦ If an older oven registers 25° low/high, then compensate by setting oven temperature 25° higher/lower.

♦ Bread baking should be stress-free. In the past I adjusted the oven temperature higher/lower for various breads and often forgot to adjust baking time accordingly. Now, I use 350° and 40 minutes for most all bread baking.

Cooling Just-Baked Bread

The baked loaf will sound hollow when tapped with a knife. Immediately turn the baked loaf from the bread pan onto a cooling rack. Otherwise, moisture from the loaf will form inside the baking pan, and make the crust moist. If the bread bottom is too light in color, allow another few minutes, or set bread under the broiler for few seconds.

If you insert a thermometer into baked bread that has just been removed from a 350° oven, you will find the moist interior temperature to be around 190°. After cooling on a rack for ten minutes, the moist interior heat is drawn to dry exterior, and the bread is ready to enjoy.

Crust

Bread just removed from the oven will feel crisp to touch. As the interior moisture leaves, and the loaf cools down, the bread crust softens.

If you prefer a crisp crust, before placing dough in the preheated oven, brush with cold water. And place a small pan of water in the oven with the dough—as the water heats it will generate steam, which encourages a crisp crust. Brush dough again with cold water after baking 20 minutes.

Check your kitchen accessory shop for oven tiles that are advertised to give bread old fashion brick-oven taste and texture, and follow the manufacturer's directions.

Oven Rising Dough

When I turn my oven on it first registers 150°, which is too hot for resting/rising dough. But some oven manufacturers have taken the bread baker into consideration and have added an area for raising the dough—a 'proofing' area where the ongoing temperature can register below 100°.

♥ *1963—In the Danby, Whitby, Yorkshire England rented home, there was a warming area above the oven that was for warming the cold dinner plates. (Years later, I realized that the oven warming area was also for proofing dough.)*

Oven Warming Dough

To warm dough that has been refrigerated prior to shaping, heat oven to 200° **and turn off oven**. Sprinkle a little flour on a baking sheet. Flatten dough, and place on baking sheet. Cover dough with a towel and place dough in the oven, with door ajar, for eight minutes. Dough should be warm enough to knead a few turns and shape into loaves.

Cold Oven Baking

To bake bread, an oven does not have to be pre-heated. When the dough is ready for the oven, place dough into a cold oven, turn the gauge to 350°, and bake for the prescribed time. Try this method when you arrive home from work and wish for fresh baked bread—aroma and flavor. Or, on summer days when you would like to keep your home cool and wish home-baked bread. Mix and knead dough the day or morning before the meal.

♥ *Late 1990s—Fresh baked cinnamon buns were cooled and immediately packed for overnight delivery to Ocala, Fl, where my childhood friend Gloria and her husband George live. The delivery driver told Gloria, "During the drive from the airport, the sweetbread smell permeated the truck."*

Pans

Pan size is important: "Presentation is everything". With the right size bread pan, bread will bake, look, slice and taste better. Cut dough to fit pan—large pan, larger portion and longer time to rise. Small buns and flat breads take less time to rise and to bake. Since the sides direct the dough, if the pan is too large, bread might flatten out and not up. The sides should be low enough for the dough to rise over the rim of the pan. This ensures a brown top crust.

My preference is a stainless steel baking pan, or a reinforced steel pan. But, I have also used glass, aluminum and throwaway aluminum foil pans.
♦ For brown sides and bottom, a glass-baking dish requires a few minutes longer baking time.
♦ For brown top crust, before placing dough into the oven, it must be raised over the rim of the baking pan.
♦ When you bake sweet buns, flatten dough with a rolling pin to about 8" x 16", and then roll as for jellyroll. This will allow 14–16 slices—more or less.
♦ If you knock a bread pan against the oven door, the dough might fall ever so slightly, and you might see slight color difference in a slice. The flavor will be just fine.
♦ Oil the baking surface (spray on oil work nice), and the bread will turn from pan without effort.

♦ To loosen bread that sticks to the baking pan, slide a knife between loaf and pan.

♦ Immediately wash baking surface with hot water, or future breads will take on an "off taste" from the oil.

♦ After washing pans, return to hot oven for immediate drying. As a reminder, keep oven door ajar. If you close the oven door, then the next time you preheat the oven, you might have to remove hot pan/pans from oven.

Pan Size

♦ Use 10" x 10" pan for 14–16 buns.

♦ A baking sheet—is good for 16–20 rolls or two bread rounds.

♦ A large 17" x 12" pan will hold 40 buns—5 across and 8 down.

♦ Use cake pans 8" or 9" for bread rounds, or for a dozen roll ups.

♦ Dark flour breads do not rise as well as white flour breads; hence the loaf has a better appearance in a smaller pan—8" x 4".

♦ A medium loaf size—8 ½" x 4 ½" pan is best for white and sweet bread.

♦ Throwaway aluminum pans are great for the new baker, but require longer baking time for a brown bottom crust.

♦ Use large loaf pans 9 ½" x 5 ½" for—four—Basic white or Basic sweet loaves from five loaf recipe. This size pan is not recommended for Basic dark-recipe flour breads.

♥ *1990s—I placed dough in a round pan that had fluted sides and a curved bottom. When baked the loaf was curved on top and bottom—a lopsided loaf.*

Perfection

The perfect loaf appeals to your senses: sound, aroma, sight along with touch and taste.

Sound—There is a cracking sound when kneading the dough and gas blisters break. There is a hollow sound when the finished loaf is tapped with a knife or thumb and forefinger.

Aroma—Place your nose to the mixture and sniff the dry ingredients. When yeast has been added and is activated, sniff the dough. After kneading dough, smell your hands. Draw in your breath and fill your lungs with aroma as bread bakes. Place your nose next to a fresh slice. The aroma is a tease to the taste buds.

Sight—The flour and liquid mixture—Yuck! Enjoy the dough as it expands. Turn on the oven light and view bread as it bakes. Enjoy the sight after bread is baked: even in texture, a not too thick crust, light in weight, and a golden brown color. When cut with a serrated knife the loaf will not collapse, but will spring into shape. There will be tiny uniform holes on each slice: each loaf is unique.

Touch—Gather the ingredients and knead the dough. Feel ingredients change from wet lumpy flour to smooth round dough. Feel the elasticity as your fingers flatten and knead dough. Sense the serrated knife slicing through a loaf. Let your eyes touch individual bread slice in anticipation.

Taste—Sample the dough. Each ingredient adds a distinct taste. Taste a middle slice, or a warm crisp end slice. Bread without butter has sweet yeasty flavor. Bread with butter is the ultimate. Convince yourself that you are taste testing.

♥ *September 23rd 2002—Ethel's Sticky Cinnamon Buns were placed into the oven. About thirty minutes later the aroma—not good—brought me to the kitchen. The buns were black—well past saving—for whatever reason the oven had been set at 500°. Ed's brother Joe was visiting with us, and he was very upset at the lost cinnamon buns.*

Planning

As a new baker, you will advance your baking skills/comfort level by first reading the suggestions for kneading, resting, rising etc. in this chapter. Plan bread making around your life style. For either one loaf or five loaves of Basic white, sweet or dark bread, set aside two hours: morning, noon, night or middle of the night. Plan ahead and have kneaded dough or baked bread in the freezer, ready for mealtime enjoyment.

Basic six ingredients are flour, milk, vegetable oil, salt, granulated sugar and yeast.
Basic six steps are mixing, kneading, resting, shaping, rising, and baking.
Basic six comments—"Delicious." "Wonderful." "Tasty," "Oh my!" "Can I have the recipe?"
And, "Did 'you'—make this?" I am never quite sure what that comment means.

First—decide on Basic white, sweet or dark-bread recipe.
(Chapter 1, 2, and 3—Basic White, Sweet and Dark Breads).
Then—read over the suggestions that might help you.
(Chapter 4—Mix, Knead, Bake and Serve)
Next—decide what ingredients you wish to use or substitute.
(Chapter 5—Ingredients that Change Basic Taste and Texture)
Finally—you are ready to consider bread toppings.
(Chapter 6—Tasty Toppings and Wholesome Meals)
In addition, for information on bread nutrition, see Reflecting on your Diet in Chapter 7.

♥ *1975s—Our Medford Lakes ranch-style home had the kitchen adjacent to the bedrooms. Since bread was made any time—day or night, the children went to sleep or awoke to bread aroma. When in 5ᵗʰ grade, Maureen wrote an essay about sleeping next to a bakery.*

Problems

If baked bread does not meet your expectations, here are a few suggestions.
♦ Bottom too light—Bread is not baked long enough.
♦ Too dense—There is not enough water, or too much flour.
♦ Split loaves—Try slashing /// dough with a knife after 40 minute rising.
♦ Bottom too dark—The bread baked too long or oven heat too high.
♦ Too many holes—The dough raised too long. Fill the holes with butter.
♦ Did not rise—If dough did not rise, purchase a room thermometer.

♦When allowing 40 minutes rising time, yeast needs an 80° area.

Oven heat that is twenty-five degrees too high or too low will make a difference.

♦Crumbly—If bread has too many crumbs, there is too much flour or not enough liquid.

♦Coarse grain—If the grain is too coarse then dough should be kneaded longer.

♦Wet inside—If bread is too moist, the dough needs longer rising or oven is too hot.

Purchase a hardware store oven thermometer, and double-check interior heat of oven.

♦Streaks in dough—The streaks can be from dough rising too close to a hot surface.

♦Too dry—If bread is too dry, bread is baked too long or has too much sugar.

♦Flat looking loaves—Dough did not raise long enough, or baking area too cold.

♦All the above—You have had too many interruptions. The next time you bake bread, allow time to enjoy the bread baking process, and to savor the results.

♥*Personal Problems—If personal problems need considering, make bread. Many an issue can be resolved by 'kneading' thoughts together. And, if the problem is not resolved, let the ingredients bake for 40 minutes. If the problem persists, you will find that warm bread and butter comforts the inner soul.*

♥*2001—While at lunch with my neighbors from Medford Lakes—Doris, Maggie, and Pat—Doris said, "My children have bread-aroma memories from living next door to Haggerty's."*

Purchasing Bread
After you have baked Basic white, sweet and/or dark bread, you will be reluctant to purchase bread. But, since it is not always convenient to bake bread, these suggestions are written to help when purchasing bread.

One hundred percent whole-wheat bread contains endosperm, germ and bran. In the nineties, the U. S. Government enforced laws on how product information should be stated on bread labels. Since wheat germ and wheat bran are brown in color, they have been removed from white bread. Because the bread manufacturer must notify customer that natural ingredients—wheat germ and wheat bran have been removed, the white bread label reads, "Reconstituted—Some natural nutrients have been removed".

What to look for when purchasing bread

When purchasing bread, experiment with different bread manufactures. Decide what nutrients are important to you and check the label. The U. S. Government suggests that we select grains for variety. Look for 100% Whole Grains: wheat, oat, rye etc. Check the label periodically for manufacturer changes.

Although manufactures advertise differently, below is a guide.

♦ When a label reads white bread, the bread is made from endosperm and without wheat bran and wheat germ. The bread is white.

♦ When a label reads whole-wheat bread, the bread is made from part white flour (endosperm) and part 100% whole-wheat flour (wheat germ and wheat bran). The bread is light tan.

♦ When a label reads 100% whole-wheat bread, the bread is made from 100% whole-wheat flour (endosperm, wheat germ and wheat bran). The bread is brown.

♦ Some mixed grain bread labels show white, whole wheat and 100% whole-wheat flour.

♦ Dark bread label might state, caramel, coffee, chocolate or food color for darkening: some bread has all.

♦ To compare home baked 100% whole wheat bread with a purchased loaf, follow the Basic dark recipe.

♥ *1987–1988—While Ed worked in Syracuse, NY, he was provided with an apartment in downtown Syracuse. Located a few blocks from the apartment was a Whole-Grain-Co-op, which six women had started. From their ever-present smiles the endeavor must have been a dream-come-true. The dark flour breads, cakes and muffins were made with the best ingredients—no additives, no bleached white flour and salt added in small amounts. To sweeten the bread they used honey, molasses, fruit or fruit juice. Customers watched the women mix, knead and place dough into a great black oven, and then stayed to inhale the bread-baking aroma. It is not always necessary to bake bread at home.*

Recipe Reading

For bread baking enjoyment read through the complete Basic white, sweet or dark bread recipe then decide the necessary ingredients: set the ingredients on the counter; check the baking area temperature; and oil the pans. As you use an ingredient, place it back into the closet. A few 'different-tasting' loaves could have been avoided, if this policy had been followed in my kitchen.

A first time baker should stay with the Basic white, sweet and dark recipe amounts. And, "not exactly" are words to keep in mind. In bread baking, it is not necessary for the ingredients, resting, rising, area warmth and baking to be exactly as called for.

The Basic one-loaf recipe suggestions can be (except, perhaps tomato pizza on sweet dough) used with Basic white, sweet and dark dough.

The Next Baking
It is "always fun" to make a loaf of bread and then to consider what ingredient to include with the next baking. Many times I check what is in the closet, refrigerator or freezer and then decide on the bread to bake.

Bake bread and buns for today, or freeze for future enjoyment. First, decide the ingredients: seeds, spice, fruit, nuts or herbs. **Next**, decide the shape: braid, buns, loaf, rolls or stolen. **Finally**, decide the pan: bread pan, tube pan, cake pan or bake sheet. For double pleasure, use two dough portions and double the additional ingredients.
When following the one-loaf suggestions, knead ingredients into the dough and bake as a loaf. Or, flatten dough and sprinkle on ingredients then roll dough and slice. To flatten dough, use rolling pin or fingers—for one loaf, measure dough about 8" x 12", which fits nicely into bread pan. For buns flatten dough to about 8" x 16". This will allow enough slices to fill a 9" round baking pan or 10" x 10" pan.

For a professional look, before placing bread into the oven, brush the dough with a fork beaten egg.

♥ *1970s–1980s—While my children—Edward, Maureen, Daniel and Anna—attended school, I kept a bread journal. I used the journals to pay attention to ingredients and to improve my bread making. And while waiting for bread to bake, I noted the day's happening—family, friends, foods etc. I regret that I scribbled my thoughts and had the open pages around the food mix, for the journals are a sad looking mess.*

♥ *2001—My granddaughter Emma informed me that she heard on television, "When someone follows a recipe they can keep a cookbook clean by covering the page with plastic wrap." When Emma looked at the many food splatters on my recipe book, she recognized the significance.*

Refrigerator
Refrigerate Dough Shaped for Bread Pans
If you enjoy baking bread for guest and enjoy good bread aroma, but do not wish to spend the time on the planned day. Place kneaded dough in bread pans, cover with towel and set in the refrigerator. Without a cover, dough will get a tough skin from dry air that circulates in the refrigerator. Either spray dough with oil and cover with plastic wrap or cover with paper or light cotton towel. While in the cold refrigerator, the bread will slowly rise. Bake within the next twenty-four hours or the dough will collapse.

♥ *January 2ⁿᵈ 2004—I had just kneaded and shaped the loaves when a neighbor made a request for my time. I placed the five Basic dark loaves: pepper, bulgur, raisin, walnut and plain—into the refrigerator with a light towel to cover. About four hours later, I returned to the house. I placed the loaves into the cold oven, set the oven for 350° and baked the loaves.*

Refrigerate Dough <u>Not</u> Shaped for bread pans
When dough is prepared for later use, first knead dough and allow 15-minute rest. Do not shape the dough. Next, wrap dough tightly and place it in the refrigerator. When ready to use, uncover, shape and cover with towel. Allow dough to rise for 40 minutes. Since refrigerated dough can get an off taste, do not keep dough longer than three days in the refrigerator. (See Freezer)

♥ *1980s—My mother-in-law told my young children that when her three sons were teenagers, and seeking food from the refrigerator, they pulled a chair to the refrigerator to have a good view. Needless to say, her grandchildren took this as a splendid suggestion.*

Resting Dough
After kneading the dough for 10 minutes, place it on floured—flat surface in an 80° area. Cover the dough and allow it to rest for 15 minutes. While the dough rests, the yeast feeds on the flour and sugar growing in number and expanding the dough with good yeast flavor. (See Rising)

In a too warm baking area, the yeast cells develop too fast, and this makes dough sticky and hard to work with. In a too cold baking area, the yeast will not develop, and this makes dough impossible to work with. It is perfectly acceptable to allow the dough to rise a few minutes too long. And if you get side tracked for too long, then press the air from the dough, shape and set to rise.

You Decide
Some bakers believe bread has better flavor if the ingredients are mixed, allowed to rest few hours in a cooler temperature and then kneaded. What does this do for taste and texture?

Rising Dough
After dough has rested (see Rested), it is greatly expanded and awkward to work with. Release the air by pushing down the dough with your hands. Shape dough and place into the appropriate pan. Cover dough with a light towel, and allow dough to rise in 80° baking area. Whether preparing a loaf or buns, allow dough about 40 minutes to rise.

If baking area is not a continuous 80°, then dough will need a longer rising time. Let your eyes be the judge. Before placing into oven, the dough should rise above the rim of the pan.

♦ Dough with all white flour will raise more once placed in the oven.

♦ The dark flour loaf will rise only a bit once placed into the oven.

♦ Should dough not rise at all, do not worry. Flatten dough with your fingers, and bake as flat bread. Serve crisp flat bread with soup and never mention otherwise.

♦ If after baking the loaf has not risen as high as it should, slice the loaf in half and then place the loaf on end and slice in the other direction. Not as many slices but nice size slices. Or, cut the loaf ¾ to ¼, and use the ¼ side to make thinly sliced toast, which is better known as Melba toast.

You Decide
Some bakers believe bread has a better flavor the longer it is allowed to raise in a cooler temperature. Experiment. Allow the dough to rest a few hours then press down the dough, and allow dough to rise again for a few hours. Shape for baking. What does this do for taste and texture?

♥ *In the late 1970s-I had this taste-memory for bread with a more yeasty flavor, and decided to try a longer rising period—overnight. On a particular May evening the windows were open, but during the night the temperature dropped drastically. A blanket kept me warm during the night, but the forgotten dough did not fare as well. In the morning the dough resembled cold glob. Ah! I thought, a bread challenge, and turned on the stovetop units to put warmth into the baking area. Three hours later the dough had raised enough for me to punch down and distribute into pans. The finished product was dry, tasteless and not worth the effort.*

Shaping—Dough

After you knead dough (see kneading), and allow it to rest (see resting) for 15 minutes, dough is ready to be shaped. You can use a rolling pin to flatten the dough, and you can use a tape measure to measure the flatten dough. But bread and buns do not have to be shaped perfect to taste delicious. Relax. Flatten dough for bread with fingers, a glass or rolling pin to about 12" x 8" or 10" x 8" or 8" x 8", or about the length and double the width of the bread pan. And flatten dough for buns to about 16" x 8". If dough shrinks, stretch it a bit from the center. When shaping dough for rolls use a knife, juice glass or biscuit cutter.

When shaping dough-

First—As you flatten the dough, judge the length of the bread pan. Roll up the dough as you would a jellyroll. When rolled, it will fit the width.

Second—Firmly roll up the dough, tuck in the ends and place seam side down in oiled baking pan.

For the buns, roll the dough and slice enough buns to fit the pan you are using. If there are extra buns bake them in a small pan.

Third—The dough should fit the pan, with enough room to rise and not look lost in the pan.

Forth—Cover the dough with a light towel, and allow it to rise in an 80° baking area for 40 minutes. If room is cool and the dough is not raised enough, allow 15 additional minutes.

Different Shapes—Basic white, sweet and dark breads

♦ Bread sticks—Flatten dough and cut into small stripes. Roll each strip back and forth between your hands until pencil thin.

♦ Bowknots—Flatten dough with a rolling pin, and cut into strips long enough to tie into bowknots.

♦ Braid—Cut dough into three equal pieces, and roll up each piece to 12" long: set pieces side by side on baking sheet. Braid dough by beginning in the center and working toward each end. Tuck the ends under and seal with water.

♦ Braided wreath—Form braided (see braid) dough into a round, seal the two ends together with water.

♦ Braided loaf—Place braided loaf in a bread pan.

♦ Braid on braid—Cut dough into four equal pieces and roll up each piece to 10" long. Braid the three pieces as for braid above. Cut remaining piece into three and roll to 5" long. Twist into a braid and place atop the larger braided loaf. Seal the dough together with small amount of water.

♦ Cake pan—Flatten dough and add nuts, or fruit then roll up dough. Cut dough into one inch slices. Place slices side by side in a 9" pan, or shape dough into a round and place into an 8" pan.

♦ Coffee can—Shape small amount of dough to fit coffee can.

♦ Crescent—Flatten dough and cut into pie shape wedges. Starting with the wide end, roll up each piece and place on baking sheet.

♦ Layered bread—Nice for ingredients such as: cranberries, mincemeat or steamed onion, which are too moist to knead into dough and can be mixed with ground nuts or toasted wheat germ. Flatten dough and place ½ ingredients down 1/3 the dough. Fold over then place ½ ingredients on top and fold over.

♦ Roll—Flatten dough and cut with a biscuit cutter or juice glass. Set rolls far apart for crisp crust; set the sides touching for soft crust.

♦ Rounds—Knead dough into a round, and bake on oiled cooking sheet that has first been sprinkled with cornmeal.

♦ Stollen—Flatten dough sprinkle with fruit and nuts, fold dough not quite in half, seal with water and place on baking sheet. When baked, cover with icing and glazed cherries.

Slashes ///

Often a new baker is uncomfortable placing a 1/16" slash (cut) down the middle or three /// slashes across the dough. When I place a loaf into the oven, I do not always remember to /// slash the dough, and many times the baked loaf shows a split on the side. This does not bother me. But, some bakers prefer an even loaf and the /// slashes direct the dough to bake evenly.

For best results, use a serrated knife. And cut with the middle of the blade as opposed to the tip of the blade.

♥ *Mid 1990s—It seemed important for me to learn how to sketch a loaf of bread. My artist friend Pat, who I first met while living in Willingboro during the sixties, offered drawing suggestions. We discussed a Basic white loaf: height, length, shade and texture. My subsequent rendition was of a fallen loaf.*

Storage

Homemade bread does not have the preservatives that commercial bread has; thus, homemade bread has a limited shelf life. Bacteria grow on homemade bread far faster than on commercial bread. For immediate use keep bread in cool dry area. For long-term freshness, freeze.

On day one, two and three home baked bread is fresh tasting.
On day four home baked bread taste fine.
On day five, six and seven, home baked bread is soft to touch and toasting enhances the good flavor.
On day eight, bread will show slight mold and has lost its fresh taste.

♦ Store crisp crust bread in a paper bag.
♦ Store soft crust bread in plastic bags that are not tightly sealed.
♦ Use grains, nuts, seeds and dried fruit shortly after purchase or store in freezer.
♦ Store bread ingredients (flour, oil, powder milk, sugar, yeast) in a cool dry place—always ready.
♦ Use a breadbox that is wood, metal or plastic, and one that has small openings for air to circulate.
♦ Before mixing, with other baking ingredients, bring freezer-stored ingredients to room temperature.
♦ The dry air that circulates in the refrigerator removes moisture from bread. For long-term keeping, store bread and bread ingredients in the freezer.
♦ Do not store bread in a tightly sealed plastic bag. The moisture from bread will be drawn out and the crust will be moist to touch and chewy to taste.

♥ *Late 1980s—On a sweet bun afternoon, Anna's friend visited. The friend's father owns a bakery, and the friend mentioned that the just-baked sweet buns did not resemble her fathers. With much effort, I left unsaid that the 'magnificent' sweet buns were made without dollar value per bun, and the buns had wholesome ingredients and no preservatives—sensitive baker.*

Substituting Ingredients

After following the Basic recipes a few times, you might wish to substitute a different ingredient.

Chapter 5—Ingredients That Change Basic Taste and Texture—gives numerous suggestions for substituting sweeteners, grains etc.

You can add or substitute a different dry ingredient—grain, fruit, seeds etc.—at step #2 of Basic recipe. Or, add or substitute different liquid ingredients—buttermilk, honey, juice etc.—at step #3 of Basic recipe.

The heartiness of 100% whole-wheat flour overpowers mild spice flavors—experiment.

♦ When substituting an ingredient, start with a small amount. You can use more/less with the next baking.

♦ When substituting a high fiber grains such as 100% whole-wheat flour or rye flour, which absorbs more liquid than white flour—add more liquid or use less flour.

♦ When substituting moist ingredients—brown sugar, honey or molasses for granulated sugar, add to heated liquid ingredients.

♦ If you wish to bake dark bread, substitute dark molasses for sweetener. And for a darker loaf add 1–2 teaspoon coffee powder or chocolate powder or both to dry ingredients.

Home-baked products might not always be professional looking, but they—most always—surpass store bought in flavor and nutrition.

♥ *June 21ˢᵗ 1986—Two tablespoons anise seeds were kneaded into one round of Basic Sweet Dough and cut as for rolls. The baked rolls were then covered with a mixture of 1-cup confections sugar, 2-tablespoons milk and 1-teaspoon anise seed. Much to the unhappiness of Daniel, the buns were taken to a picnic at my God Daughter Gloria Ann's home.*

Temperature

My secret to successful bread baking is thermometers: room, liquid and oven. Yes, I have shared the secret to successful bread baking throughout the book. And, by now you are tired reading about room, liquid and oven temperature, but this secret eliminates most bread baking problems.

Growing yeast cells need warmth, and do not recover well from area or ingredients that are too hot or too cold. To someone new at baking bread, or someone who tried bread baking with poor results, bread baking might seem a great secret. The bread baker who follows well-written directions and keeps the bread-making area around 80° knows the bread-baking secret.

Purchase a room thermometer for inexpensive visual assurance. After many years, my room thermometer broke. I did not bother to replace it until I realized that the bread loaves did not rise as high as usual. My kitchen is about 70° and that is not warm enough to raise dough in 40 minutes. A room thermometer keeps me aware that I must turn on the stove units for the immediate bread baking area to be close to 80°. The baking area might be uncomfortable warm to you, but not to the yeast. To encourage warmth in the area, when you decide to bake bread, immediately turn on the oven.

Purchase a liquid thermometer solely for testing liquid ingredients. A liquid thermometer will give an instant read and take the guessing from bread making.

Purchase an oven thermometer for reassurance. If your oven is not dependable, an oven thermometer is reassuring.

The temperature, room, liquid and oven, does not have to register exactly at the recipe recommended degree.

♥ *During the 1960s—When I first baked bread, the liquid was tested by sprinkling on my wrist—if too hot for the wrist then too hot for the yeast—it worked.*

♥ *In the 1970s—An advertisement in a food magazine for marvelous 'Secret Crackling Bread', enticed me to send a check. By return mail, I received a 4" x 2" index card with the 'Secret crackling Recipe'. With each check received for a 4" x 2" index card, the seller must wear a secret smile.*

Time Necessary
In bread books written 100 years ago, authors recommended that bread making be started in the evening, and the dough allowed to rise overnight. In bread books written thirty years ago, authors recommend three to five hours for rising dough. This bread book recommends 40 minutes for rising dough.

Basic bread—two hours—white, sweet and dark
10 minutes—mix ingredients-
10 minutes—knead dough-
15 minutes—rest dough—
5 minutes—shape dough and place into pan-
40 minutes—raise dough and to allow flavors to develop—
40 minutes—bake loaves—

While dough rest, the baker can clean mixing containers and prepare baking pan. While dough rises, bakes and cools, the baker can read, watch television, talk on the telephone, check e-mail etc.
When the bread is baked you have bread for immediately enjoyment. And if you have followed the five-loaf recipe then you have bread for family, friends and freezer.

Timer—When I bake white, sweet and dark bread on the same day, there are many timers going. When baking bread, my kitchen is organized disorder.

♥ *December 20th 1993—Anna followed the five-loaf Basic bread recipe, and made ten small loaves of raisin bread to give as gifts to coworkers. When the magnificent loaves were baked, I question, "Will you make bread again?" "Yes." Anna answered, "That was fun."*

Utensils
There are utensils necessary for baking bread: there are utensils convenient to have.
Utensils Necessary
♦ An oven-temperature gauge—An oven temperature gauge is reassuring.
♦ Baking pans—Stainless-steel baking pans are good heat conductors.
♦ Cooling rack—To allow air to circulate around just baked bread, use a cooling rack.
♦ Large pot—A large pot to heat liquid.

♦ Measuring cup—Fill aluminum-measuring cups with flour and level off with the back of a knife.

♦ Measuring spoons—Measuring spoons are great for salt and spice.

♦ Mixing bowl—Use mixing bowls to hold ingredients.

♦ Mixing spoon—Use mixing spoon to blend ingredients.

♦ Serrated knife—A serrated knife is a must for cutting through dough and slicing bread.

♦ Thermometers—Use a bread thermometer for testing liquid, and a room thermometer for visual assurance.

More Utensils Utensils that are not necessary for bread baking but convenient to have.

♦ Bags—Food storage bags 11 ½" x 12 ½" are ideal for loaves 8" x 4" or 8 ½" x 4 ½". And bags 13" x 15" are great for one 9" x 5" loaf, or two 8" x 4" loaves.

♦ Baking sheets—Use 10" x 13" baking sheet for two rounds or a long braided loaf.

♦ Biscuit cutter—Biscuit cutters are sold in a unit—small, medium and large.

♦ Cake pans—Use 8" or 9" cake pan for sweet roll ups, sweet buns or a full round.

♦ Cutting board—Use wood or plastic.

♦ Cast Iron—Cast iron pans were the choice for cooking over open fire, and preferred by many cooks today.

♦ Dough hook—The dough hook works well with one-loaf Basic recipe.

♦ Food chopper—A food chopper takes up little room for great results: nuts, mince cranberries etc.

♦ Juice extractor—Try substituting fruit or vegetable juice for some liquid in Basic recipe.

♦ Pastry brush—A pastry brush is handy for applying glaze to small buns, cold water to dough and for greasing baking pans. Fingers are a fine substitute.

♦ Potholders—Keep potholders away from moisture, and throw away potholders with holes.

♦ Rolling pin—To flatten dough use a rolling pin, a jar, a drinking glass—your fingers

♦ Scale—A scale is perfect for measuring flour. Too often you will start counting out the flour cups only to be distracted. A scale never leaves you wondering. When following the five loaf Basic recipe use a scale to evenly divide the dough.

♦ Scissors—Scissors are handy for opening dry yeast packets.

♦ Scraper—When the counter top is sticky with dough, use a scraper to immediately clear away the mess.

♦ Spray bottle—A spray water bottle is nice when baking crusty breads. For a dark, crisp crust, spray dough with water before baking and half way through baking.

♦ Terra Cotta pans—For old world, brick oven taste and texture some bakers recommend terra cotta pans.

♦ Timer—If easily distracted, a timer is invaluable. While bread is baking, a timer can travel with you to other rooms.

♦ Toaster—For enjoyment, toasted homemade bread competes with just baked bread.

♦ Toast rack—A toast rack, keeps toast separated and air can circulated—thus crisp toast.

♥ *Early 1990s—I am from the "If it works don't change it" school, which is not always the best school. For years, I used a knife to chop ingredients that were necessary for baking. After Anna gave me a food chopper, my recipe possibilities extended: ground nuts, chopped cranberries and fine breadcrumbs to name a few.*

♥ *There are three rolling pins in my home—my mother's, my Aunt Rose's, and my grandchildren's, which measures 8" and requires a child's concentration to use.*

♥ *March 5th, 2002—A large serving spoon, stored in the kitchen drawer, has many holes for straining off liquid. My granddaughter, Rebecca who was born in '99 and just tall enough to see into the drawer, said, "Funny spoon."*

Yeast—In Bread Baking

Years ago we 'proofed' yeast (microscopic plant) by mixing it with warm water and sugar to feed on. After 10 minutes the mixture would foam—the yeast was activated. Now yeast packages are dated, and can be purchased with confidence. Dry yeast does not need to be 'proofed'.

Dry yeast, when purchased for bread baking, is deactivated and not killed. To activate dry yeast for basic recipes, mix yeast for about one minute with dry ingredients then combine with 130° liquids.

When yeast is mixed, with Basic bread ingredients (warm liquid, flour and salt) the yeast produces a gas—carbon dioxide—that along with gluten in the flour expands the dough. The more dough is kneaded, the more the yeast is distributed and the more the dough expands.

Additional yeast speeds the yeast rising action and gives bread a more yeasty flavor. Too much yeast can make dough sticky and difficult to work with. Active dry yeast—in the proper amount—gives bread good flavor, delicious aroma and makes bread light and airy.

Yeast—Fine Grain Faster Rising
At the supermarket there are two types of dry yeast—fine grain and a heavy grain. The Basic bread recipes in this book call for the fine grain yeast sold as Faster Rising Highly 'Active Dry Yeast'. The fine grain in this yeast more readily distributes evenly throughout the flour, and when activated by 130° liquids, the dough rises faster.

Although the heavy grain yeast in the other type 'Active Dry Yeast' is recommended for six, nine and twelve-hour dough rising recipes, it is also acceptable to use with Basic recipes. The dough might need to rise longer. Let your eyes be the judge.

Yeast Guessing removed
♦ Allow time for yeast to multiply.
♦ Have flour, sugar etc. in proportion to yeast.
♦ Water that is too hot will kill yeast.
♦ If water is too cold, yeast will not be activated.
♦ If baking area is too hot, dough will be sticky.
♦ If baking area is too cold, dough will take forever to rise or not rise at all.
♦ If too little yeast is used, dough will not rise enough.
♦ If too much yeast, dough will rise too fast and have a bitter taste.

There is Solace in Ritual

5

Ingredients that Change Bread Taste and Texture

Ingredients that Change Bread Taste and Texture—
Shown in this chapter are ingredients that change bread taste and texture—Eggs, Extracts/Flavorings, Fats, Fruits, Grains, Herbs, Liquids, Nuts, Organic Ingredients, Salt, Seeds, Spices, Sweeteners and Yeast.

Follow the Basic bread recipe a few times, and then consider changing the bread taste and/or texture. Substitute a dry ingredient at Basic bread recipe step #2, or, substituting a liquid ingredient at Basic bread recipe step #3. Or, while kneading the dough, knead fruit, nuts etc. into the dough. The suggested amounts, for one-loaf recipe, are shown with the ingredient.

Nutrition
The nutrition in the measured amount, is as listed on manufactures packaging or U. S. Government publications. The nutrition in particular ingredients varies from grams, milligrams and trace amounts. An ingredient might show 'trace' amounts in ¼ cup, but will measure differently in 1-cup filled with the same ingredient.

The nutrition value—Calories, Carbohydrate, Fat, Protein, Sodium and Dietary Fiber shown with each ingredient is an approximate count for the baker and is not to be used to establish personal health or weight gain/loss. For additional nutritional information refer to the "U. S. Government Nutritive Value of Foods" Home and Garden Bulletin Number 72, or product packages.

Eggs

Eggs give bread structure, color, tenderness and flavor. For best results have eggs at room temperature.

For rich brown color and high gloss, brush fork beaten egg on bread, buns or rolls before baking.

	Calories	Carbohydrate	Fat	Protein	Sodium	Fiber
1-Egg	75	1 g	5 g	6 g	63 mg	0

♦ Eggshells are porous and should not contact high flavored food in the refrigerator.

♦ Before sprinkling dough with caraway or sesame seeds, brush dough with fork-beaten egg white.

♥ *April 15th 2001—At our annual Easter brunch, scrambled eggs were on the menu, and to keep the eggs warm, they were placed into an electric warming pan. After a short while, the eggs turned green. This had Edward speculating, "Where did (Theodore Geisel) Dr. Seuss come up with the idea for his book, "Green Eggs and Ham"?*

Extracts and Flavoring

Food extracts and flavorings give a tantalizing taste to bread and bread toppings. Follow the Basic recipe, and add a pinch or a drop with other ingredients, knead onto dough, or blend into icing.

Food extracts and flavorings contribute insignificant amounts of nutrition.

Experiment with extracts and flavorings such as, Anise, Banana, Black Walnut, Brandy, Butter, Cherry, Chocolate, Coconut, Lemon, Maple, Orange, Pineapple, Raspberry, Rum, Strawberry, Vanilla etc.

♦ Add 1-teaspoon extract per 4-cups flour.

♦ Extracts lose their full flavor when frozen in baked breads.

♦ Mix 1-teaspoon vanilla extract with ½-cup sugar. This is luscious sprinkled on warm toast.

♦ Extracts and flavorings that are more than a year old, or left without a cover, lose their full flavor.

♦ Vanilla sugar: split one long vanilla bean and remove seeds. Mix vanilla bean and seeds into 1-cup of brown or white sugar, cover and set aside for a week.

Fat
Fat, when blended with yeast and flour, gives elasticity to dough, and helps make bread soft, moist and tender. Most bread recipes include butter, lard, margarine, olive oil or vegetable oil.

For nutrition, flavor and convenience, the Basic bread recipes—white, sweet and dark—call for vegetable oil.

♦ For fat free bread, eliminate vegetable oil and milk from Basic recipe, and increase the water accordingly.
♦ To keep rolls from baking together, spray-oil the rolls touching side.
♦ To keep dough from sticking to the pan, spray-oil the baking surface (spray oil works nice).

♥ *Early 1900s—For ease in pouring honey or molasses, Ed's grandmother first measured lard or butter into a cup then used the same cup to measure sticky ingredients. The ingredients poured from the cup with ease.*

♥ *1940's—As children Ed and his brothers lived in their grandparent's house. Ed's mother worked for H. Freeman and Son as a telephone operator. The boys did the house chores on Friday and on Friday night their mother brought Philadelphia Cinnamon buns home for dessert.*

Butter
Warm butter on sweet bread is mouth-watering; cold butter on warm toast is tantalizing. For a different flavor and rich color, in Basic sweet-bread recipe, replace vegetable oil with equal amount of butter.

	Calories	Carbohydrate	Fat	Protein	Sodium	Fiber
¼-cup	408	trace	48 g	trace	468 mg	0

♦ Low fat butter is made from skim milk and gelatin.
♦ 4-tablespoons = ¼-cup/1-stick butter = ½ cup/2-sticks butter = ½-pound.
♦ When adding dry ingredients such as cinnamon/sugar mixture to dough, flatten dough and brush with soft butter, and firmly roll up dough. Without the butter the baked bread will unravel when sliced.

♥ *March 1993—Each week my local newspaper, "Central Record", provides readers with a look back to happenings published 25 or 50 years ago.*
The publication dated 3/4/43, discussed rationing books issued and price ceilings for products. Butter to be priced no higher than 57 cents a pound (58 cents if delivered), and grade A eggs (large) priced 53 cents a pound.

Canola Oil
Use canola oil in place of vegetable oil in the Basic recipes.

	Calories	Carbohydrate	Fat	Protein	Sodium	Fiber
¼-cup	496	0	56 g	0	0	0

Lard
Because lard adds no color and keeps cost down many commercial bakeries use lard in bread baking. Substitute equal amounts lard for vegetable oil in Basic recipes.

	Calories	Carbohydrate	Fat	Protein	Sodium	Fiber
¼-cup	460	0	52 g	0	trace	0

Margarine
Margarine is made from vegetable oil, skim milk and other ingredients. Substitute equal amounts margarine for vegetable oil in Basic recipe.

	Calories	Carbohydrate	Fat	Protein	Sodium	Fiber
¼-cup	404	trace	44 g	trace	528 mg	0

♥ *Early 1940s—During World WW 2, grocery products such as butter and sugar were necessary for the men fighting in Europe. In the U. S. this created a shortage. Such items were then purchased with stamps from food rationing book along with money. The government provided each family with ration books in accordance to family size. Oleomargarine was immediately sold as a butter substitute, and was available without food rationing stamps. The white Oleomargarine, which resembled lard, was sold with an orange/yellow color packet. The homemaker blended the color into the soft oleomargarine for the resulting butter-look.*

Olive Oil
The olive oils at the market are virgin, extra virgin, light, extra light, pure, and 100% olive oil. The label on the olive oil container that I use for bread baking (and cake making) reads 'Full Bodied and Mild Tasting—100% Natural All-purpose Cooking Oil'. This extra light olive oil is pale golden in color.
See Vegetable Oil.

The label on the olive oil that I use for bread dip, reads 'Extra Virgin Olive Oil'. The oil is green in color, and when blended with herbs make a tasty bread dip.

	Calories	Carbohydrate	Fat	Protein	Sodium	Fiber
¼-cup	476	0	56 g	0	trace	0

♥ *May 1990—To celebrate Mother's day, I went with Maureen and Anna to Victor's Restaurant in South Philadelphia. While the waiters sang arias from various operas, we celebrated with a magnificent meal: warm bread served with hot olive oil, garlic and herbs followed by lasagna with just a hint of nutmeg. And for dessert' we enjoyed crème Brule, an egg pudding with burnt sugar topping.*

Vegetable Oil
Because vegetable oil is more accessible to the bread baker, the Basic white, sweet and dark recipes call for vegetable oil.
See Olive Oil.

	Calorie	Carbohydrate	Fat	Protein	Sodium	Fiber
¼-cup	480	0	56 g	0	0	0

♥ *1980s—Before placing dough into the oven, I sprayed a loaf with vegetable oil and sprinkled on sesame seeds. When the loaf was removed from the oven, sesame seeds slide off the loaf like sand.*
Lesson learned: Brush the loaf with egg white and then add seeds.

Fruit
Fresh Fruit
While most fresh fruit is too moist for bread baking, whole, chopped or crushed fresh fruits are great served with bread. Fruit sauces and butters are delicious bread toppings; and fruit chunks are good on fruit pizza.

♦ For fresh berry goodness blend ½ cup water with 1-cup sugar, and then add 1-quart berries (strawberry, raspberry, blueberry) and cook for a few minutes.
♦ Crush 1-pint berries with 1-tablespoon sugar. No cooking necessary.
♦ Top morning toast or lather warm bread slice with berry goodness; wear a bib and have paper towels available. (See Chapter 6 for Tasty Toppings.)

Dry Fruit

Dry fruits are high in taste, texture, fiber, calories and carbohydrates. Dry fruits are low in fat; most have no fat. Dry fruit adds color to white, sweet or dark bread.
♦ When adding dry fruit to Basic bread ingredients or to bread dough, have dry fruit at room temperature. ♦ If you like a little fruit with your bread, allow one cup dry fruit to four cups flour.
♦ If you like little bread with your fruit, add 2-cups fruit per four cups flour.

Apples

Dry apples are mild tasting. Before adding apples to Basic sweet-bread recipe dough, blend 1-teaspoon cinnamon with 1-tablespoon sugar and mix with 1-cup chopped dried apples.

	Calorie	Carbohydrate	Fat	Protein	Sodium	Fiber
¼-cup	125	25 g	0	0	10 mg	2 g

♥ *July 29ᵗʰ 1984—Anna and Maureen are in Florida visiting with Gloria, George and family. I followed the Basic sweet bread recipe with the addition of dried apples. The resulting flavor was hardly worth the effort. A bit of cinnamon or nutmeg would have helped.*

♥ *1979—On a summer evening, we went for a walk with our guest, Eleanor. (I worked with Eleanor at the DuPont Company in Wynnewood, PA during the 1950s.) We left the dishes and the unfinished apple cake on the porch picnic table. And when we returned from our walk we found Brandy, the Irish setter from next-door, enjoying the remaining cake. We were particularly fond of Brandy and found great humor in this sight. Eleanor found no humor—she had made the apple cake. Brandy was a regular visitor to our house. He stopped by to see Daniel, but if encouraged he would stay and find a comfortable place on the floor at the kitchen door.*

Apricots
One cup chopped dried apricots is a tangy, tasty addition to the Basic dough.

	Calorie	Carbohydrate	Fat	Protein	Sodium	Fiber
¼-cup	107	25 g	0	1 g	1 mg	2 g

Cherries
Dried cherries are close in flavor to fresh cherries. Knead 1-cup dried cherries into Basic white, sweet or dark recipe dough.

	Calorie	Carbohydrate	Fat	Protein	Sodium	Fiber
¼-cup	120	32 g	0	0	10 mg	3 g

Cranberry
Cranberry bread serves as an elegant centerpiece for holidays: color, flavor and nutrition. Use 1-cup dry sweetened cranberry to 4-cups flour.

	Calories	Carbohydrate	Fat	Protein	Sodium	Fiber
¼-cup	105	24 g	0	0	0 mg	3 g

♦ Mix ½-cup cranberries, and ½ cup nuts with dough for a tart and tasty crunch.

♥ *December 12th 1984—I followed the Basic sweet bread recipe for five loaves with tasty additions: two cups holiday fruit, 4-cups walnuts, 2-cups fresh cranberries and 2-cups raisins. Amazing all that fruit, yet not enough fruit. Because the cranberries used were fresh cranberries, the loaves are a bit too moist in the center. It would have been better to use dry cranberries.*

Currants
This small seedless raisin—currant—adds unusual taste and texture to Basic dark bread. Soften currants by marinating 1-cup currants with 2-tablespoons cooking sherry for two hours, drain well and knead into Basic dark-recipe dough.
Serve this rich, moist satisfying bread with coffee after dinner.

	Calories	Carbohydrates	Fat	Protein	Sodium	Fiber
¼-cup	105	27 g	0	1 g	7 mg	2 g

Dates

Dates have a soft, sweet flavor and are exotic tasting in bread. Knead 1-cup chopped dates into Basic sweet or dark recipe dough.

	Calories	Carbohydrate	Fat	Protein	Sodium	Fiber
¼-cup	123	33 g	0	1 g	1 mg	3 g

Glazed fruit

At holiday time, the supermarkets sell mixed glazed fruit: orange, lemon, lime, cherries and pineapple. To one loaf recipe add 1-cup mixed glazed fruit.

	Calories	Carbohydrate	Fat	Protein	Sodium	Fiber
¼-cup	200	50 g	0	0	40 mg	2 g

♦ Drizzle baked holiday bread with ½ cup powder sugar mixed with 1-tablespoon water and top with whole nuts and glazed cherries.

Peaches

When added to sweet bread, dried peaches are a natural sweet that take on a favorable change. Knead 1-cup chopped peaches into Basic sweet-bread recipe dough.

	Calories	Carbohydrate	Fat	Protein	Sodium	Fiber
¼-cup	100	25 g	0	2 g	0 mg	3 g

Prunes

Before kneading 1-cup prunes into dough, chop and mix the prunes, and then mix with 1-teaspoon of flour. This helps to keep moist prune pieces from sticking together.

	Calories	Carbohydrate	Fat	Protein	Sodium	Fiber
¼-cup	110	26 g	0	1 g	5 mg	2 g

♥ *Many will question your wisdom in serving prune bread; but prune bread has its own fans—young and old.*

Raisins

Dark raisins are the most recognized and accepted dried fruit to family and friends, young and old. Golden raisins are sweeter tasting than dark raisins yet less recognized. Mix ½-cup golden raisins with ½-cup dark raisins and knead into Basic sweet-bread recipe dough.

Dark Raisins

	Calories	Carbohydrate	Fat	Protein	Sodium	Fiber
¼-cup	130	31 g	0	1 g	10 mg	2 g

Golden Raisins

	Calories	Carbohydrate	Fat	Protein	Sodium	Fiber
¼ cup	125	33 g	0	1 g	12 mg	1 g

♦ Two slices Basic white bread, 2-tablespoons peanut butter, and 2-tablespoons raisins—Now that's a sandwich.

♥ *1990s—As a social worker in Camden County, NJ, I attended many office celebrations. And at each celebration, sweet and savory breads found acceptance with all. Now that I am retired, when I meet a coworker, bread is remembered.*

Plump raisins

To plump raisins, add 1-cup raisins to 1-cup boiling water. Turn off unit, and allow raisins to set for an hour. Drain and use the liquid toward the measured recipe liquid. Add the moist raisins with the recipe liquid. Because raisins darken the water, this method darkens the flour but adds to the flavor.

♥ *1930s–1950s—My* mother-in-law said that when her mother made raisin-bread, she first 'plumped' the raisins.

Grains

Some whole grain products are amaranth, barley, bran, bulgur, cracked wheat, quinoa, raw wheat, rolled wheat, soy, wheat berry, wheat germ, and 100% whole-wheat.

Some wheat products are bleached and unbleached flour, cake flour, pre-sifted/not-sifted flour, pastry flour, self-rising flour, bread flour and all-purpose flour. Is it any wonder the baker gets confused?

If a particular grain cannot be found in the supermarket, request it, or check a health food store. If your health food store does not have a fast turnover you could purchase stale grains. While hardly noticed in the store, stale grains make home baked bread taste stale: a great disappointment. If products are dusty or not cared for, buy elsewhere.

♦ Because grains are high in fat, they have a short shelf life. Use shortly after purchase or keep in the freezer.

♦ To bring frozen grains to room temperature, place in microwave oven for a few seconds.

All-purpose White flour
Because all-purpose white flour is the most available flour on supermarket shelf, it is recommended for use in Basic white and sweet bread recipes.

	Calories	Carbohydrate	Fat	Protein	Sodium	Fiber
¼-cup	100	22 g	0	3 g	0	0 g

♥ *1960s–2000s—A major part of my bread baking, is experimenting with whole grains. For the new baker, the Basic-bread recipe in this book removes the guesswork. And with the recommended ingredient amounts in this chapter, the new and experienced baker can use whole grain ingredients with confidence.*

♥ *Late 1960s—The children's play area in our Levit-built home, included closets that were for toys and games and closets for pots and pans. In fact, there were more closets than a new homemaker could fill. One afternoon the children strayed to a closet where the flour was stored. Seeing toddlers have fun with flour taught this mother what to keep on the top shelf.*

Amaranth

For breakfast, lunch, dinner and snack, we eat bread that is familiar to us. For a change, consider Amaranth, which makes mealtime bread flavorful. To soften amaranth, bring ½-cup water to a boil, remove from heat, and add ½ cup amaranth, cover and let set 15 minutes. Since the grain is then moist, add to liquid before adding to dry ingredients. Substitute ½-cup soften amaranth for ½ cup flour in Basic white, sweet or dark flour recipe.

	Calories	Carbohydrate	Fat	Protein	Sodium	Fiber
¼-cup	200	35 g	3 g	8 g	0	2 g

Barley

Barley is a grain used as a food and in making beer and whiskey. Cook ½-cup barley with 1-cup water for 10 minutes. For extra texture and nutrition, substitute ½-cup well-drained barley into the liquid for bread making and then add to dry ingredients.

	Calories	Carbohydrate	Fat	Protein	Sodium	Fiber
¼-cup	170	37 g	1 g	5 g	0	5 g

♥ *September 20th 1986—I cooked barley and mixed it with other liquid ingredients and then added lentil and wheat. Maureen said, "Best bread ever." But while mixing the ingredients, such comments—yuck etc.*

Bleached flour

All-purpose flour is bleached and enriched flour—See all-purpose flour.

	Calories	Carbohydrate	Fat	Protein	Sodium	Fiber
¼-cup	100	22 g	0	3 g	0	0

Bran—Wheat
Wheat bran, the outer cover of the wheat germ, is high in dietary fiber. For additional fiber and flavor, substitute ½-cup wheat bran in Basic recipe.

	Calories	Carbohydrate	Fat	Protein	Sodium	Fiber
¼-cup	26	8 g	0	3 g	0	6 g

Bran Toasted

	Calories	Carbohydrate	Fat	Protein	Sodium	Fiber
¼ cup	30	10 g	1 g	3 g	0	7 g

Bread flour
Use flour labeled Bread Flour in Basic white and sweet bread making. More often 'Bread Flour' cannot be found in the supermarket, therefore the Basic recipes in this book call for all-purpose flour, which is available at all food markets.

	Calories	Carbohydrate	Fat	Protein	Sodium	Fiber
¼-cup	100	22 g	0	4 g	0	1 g

Buckwheat
Substitute ½ cup buckwheat flour in Basic dark recipe. Buckwheat has a distinct flavor.

	Calories	Carbohydrate	Fat	Protein	Sodium	Fiber
¼-cup	100	21 g	1 g	4 g	0	3 g

Bulgur wheat
Bulgur—the whole-wheat berry can be softened before adding to a recipe. For scant cup (not well cooked) bulgur, bring ½ cup water to a boil, add ½-cup bulgur, turn off heat and allow to 20 to 30 minutes or according to desired 'bite'. Substitute ½-cup bulgur in Basic dark recipe.

	Calories	Carbohydrate	Fat	Protein	Sodium	Fiber
¼-cup	140	30 g	0	5 g	5 mg	7 g

♦ For additional bite, knead ½ cup dry bulgur into Basic dark dough.

♥*March 19th '2004—I had bulgur in the freezer and heated it for one minute to take away the chill. I then added 3-cups bulgur to the Basic 5-loaf dark recipe. This bread is nice when fresh baked. It will taste even better when toasted and the bulgur bits are warm and crisp.*

Cake flour
Cake flour is a many times sifted white flour that gives cake a light texture. It is not recommended for bread baking. An advertisement for cake flour, in a cookbook published in early 1900s, states that cake flour is "27 times as fine as bread flour".

	Calories	Carbohydrates	Fat	Protein	Sodium	Fiber
¼-cup	100	23 g	0	2 g	0	0

Cracked wheat
See Bulgur—Cracked wheat is whole-wheat berry cracked. It has a nice 'bite' when added without first cooking. To cook cracked wheat before mixing with other ingredients, bring ½ cup water to a boil; and add ½ cup cracked wheat. Turn off heat and allow mixture to set for five minutes.

Cornmeal
Cornmeal (yellow or white—fine or granular) blends well with dark flour. Substitute ¼-cup in Basic one-loaf dark recipe. Corn meal flavor can be overwhelming, experiment with small amounts.

	Calories	Carbohydrate	Fat	Protein	Sodium	Fiber
¼-cup	100	22 g	1 g	3 g	0	3 g

♦ Sprinkle corn meal on a towel and roll dough-loaf back and forth onto the corn meal. Place on a baking sheet and allow 40 minutes to rise.
♦ For a tasty bottom crust, sprinkle cornmeal onto the baking sheet.

♥*1970s—I substituted too much cornmeal, and disliked the overpowering cornmeal flavor bread. Many negative comments.*

♥*February 1st 1987—Snow is covering the ground and reflecting sunlight. Daniel is out camping in the beautiful cold snow. Today's bread combines—white flour, 100% whole wheat, soy, rye, barley, oats and cornmeal. Delicious.*

Enriched white flour

According to government regulations, all-purpose white flour manufacturers must replace vitamins and minerals that were removed with the wheat germ and bran. The flour label must read 'Enriched White Flour'. (This government regulation also applies to bread manufacturers.)

Gluten

If you take flour and wash away the starch, what remains is gluten. Gluten is a protein found in wheat, oat, buckwheat and barley; wheat has the most. Rye has little gluten, and soy, corn and millet flour have no gluten. For a light high loaf, add 1-tablespoon gluten to 4-cups flour.

	Calories	Carbohydrate	Fat	Protein	Sodium	Fiber
¼-cup	140	12 g	0	20 g	0	0

Graham flour

Graham flour is 100% whole-wheat flour with coarse bran. Use graham flour in Basic dark recipe.

	Calories	Carbohydrate	Fat	Protein	Sodium	Fiber
¼-cup	100	22 g	1 g	3 g	0	3 g

Millet

Millet is a grass cultivated for eatable seed. Millet flour will darken white-flour bread. Substitute 1-cup millet flour in Basic dark recipe.

	Calories	Carbohydrate	Fat	Protein	Sodium	Fiber
¼-cup	210	40 g	3 g	6 g	0	5 g

Oats

Purchase oats that are sold for breakfast oatmeal, and substitute ½ cup oats to Basic recipe flour.

	Calories	Carbohydrate	Fat	Protein	Sodium	Fiber
¼-cup	75	13 g	1 g	2 g	0	2 g

◆ Mix ½ cup oats with ¼ cup brown sugar. Brush 3-tablespoons butter on flattened Basic sweet or dark recipe dough, sprinkle on oats, firmly roll up dough and place in bread pan.

♥*February 23ʳᵈ, 1987—The 'big snow', and I made bread with 100% whole wheat, oats and barley. The bread has good taste. Bread baking/experimenting is fun on a day that snow is keeping me indoors.*

Oat Bran Flour Blend
Many manufacturers combine flours, which make for tasty breads. Substitute 1-cup flour blend in Basic recipe.

	Calories	Carbohydrate	Fat	Protein	Sodium	Fiber
¼ cup	110	24 g	1 g	3 g	0	3 g

Pre-sifted flour
Pre-sifted flour is much lighter than all-purpose flour and is not recommended for bread baking.

Pastry Flour
Pastry flour has a firm texture, but less gluten, and is not recommended for Basic bread recipes. Use pastry flour for pastry, cakes and cookies.

Pumpernickel
Dense dark pumpernickel bread is made from rye flour—with or without the addition of whole-wheat flour—and darkeners: molasses, dark corn syrup, coffee and/or chocolate. Each darkener, in small amounts, will give bread a rich color without heavy ingredient flavor.

♦ Caraway seeds, when added to dough, make hearty tasting pumpernickel bread.
♦ For a professional bottom crust, sprinkle 2-tablespoons cornmeal on oiled baking sheet.

♥*February 5ᵗʰ 1984—I made pumpernickel bread with too much chocolate for darkener. It tasted like chocolate bread. It is best to combine darkeners: chocolate, molasses and coffee. This is the first time that I ever found chocolate distasteful.*

Quinoa

Quinoa gives a pleasant and nutritious change to bread flavor. Eat by the bowl full or blend into Basic bread recipe. For ½-cup soft quinoa bring ¼ cup water to a boil, remove from heat, and add ¼-cup quinoa, cover and let set for 15 minutes. Add to the liquid and then blend into the dry ingredients.

	Calories	Carbohydrate	Fat	Protein	Sodium	Fiber
¼-cup	169	28 g	2 g	5 g	8 mg	3

Raw whole-wheat

For a rough texture, substitute 1-cup 100% ground raw wheat in Basic dark recipe without prior softening.

	Calories	Carbohydrate	Fat	Protein	Sodium	Fiber
¼-cup	100	13 g	0	4 g	1 mg	4 g

Rolled Whole-wheat

Rolled whole wheat is good when served as breakfast cereal and when sprinkled atop sliced buttered bread.

	Calories	Carbohydrate	Fat	Protein	Sodium	Fiber
¼-cup	60	15	1 g	2 g	0	2 g

Rye Flour

Rye flour is milled from whole rye kernel. Because the whole rye kernel is high in oil, it has a short shelf life. As with all whole grains, store rye flour in the freezer. Substitute 1-cup rye flour for 1-cup whole-wheat flour.

	Calories	Carbohydrate	Fat	Protein	Sodium	Fiber
¼-cup	90	22 g	1 g	3 g	0	5 g

◆ Rye flour alone makes dense, heavy bread with full body flavor.
◆ For all-around crust, shape rye dough into rounds and bake on baking sheet.
◆ Rye flour has little gluten—for a sizable loaf mix—rye, wheat and white flour.
◆ For darker bread, add 1-teaspoons instant coffee and 1-teaspoons baking chocolate.
◆ Rye flour bread with caraway seeds and/or grated orange peel has a distinct flavor.
◆ For a tasty bottom crust, sprinkle 2-tablespoons corn meal onto the baking sheet.

♥*March 5ᵗʰ 1984—I added 1-tablespoon powdered chocolate and 1-tablespoon powdered coffee to 5-loaf recipe with 100% whole wheat and rye flour. The resulting five loaves have good flavor and rich color.*

Self-Rising Flour
Self-rising flour contains salt and baking soda. This flour gives best results when the recipe itself specifies self-rising flour. Self-rising flour is not suitable for Basic yeast bread recipes.

♥*June 15ᵗʰ 1992—The cake flour for Anna's birthday cake had been purchased in haste by container size, color and shape and not by brand name. It is not cake flour, but self-rising flour, which includes salt and baking soda. The cake recipe I followed called for additional salt and baking soda. This resulted is a low, salty and unappetizing layer cake.*

Soy Flour
Soy flour is made from ground soybeans. Soy flour has no gluten and bread made with soy flour will not rise without adding white flour, or 100% whole-wheat flour. Soy flour gives a pale yellow color to bread with little flavor change. Substitute 1-cup soy flour for white or dark flour in Basic recipe.

	Calories	Carbohydrate	Fat	Protein	Sodium	Fiber
¼-cup	100	8 g	5 g	8 g	0	4 g

♥*1980s—A meat loaf recipe that I followed called for soy as a high protein hamburger helper. I followed the recipe, and found that the usual throw away fat drippings were not in the pan. The unhealthy fat had been absorbed into the healthy high fiber soy.*

Stone Ground Whole Wheat—See Whole Wheat.

Tabouli—See Bulgur or Cracked Wheat.

Toasted Cracked Wheat—See Bulgur.

Triticale—Triticale combines whole-wheat flour and rye flour.

Unbleached flour
If family or friends recognize white bread for being pure white, you will have to explain why the bread has pale brown coloring. Unbleached flour has the yellow to pale brown look from trace amounts wheat germ and wheat bran. It makes great tasting bread.

	Calories	Carbohydrate	Fat	Protein	Sodium	Fiber
¼-cup	100	22 g	0	3 g	0	1 g

Uncracked Bulgur—See wheat berry.

Wheat Berry
Wheat berry is the combined endosperm, bran and germ and is also referred to as uncracked bulgur or wheat berry. Soften ½ cup whole-wheat berry in hot water before substituting in Basic dark bread recipe.

Wheat Germ—not toasted
Wheat germ is the smallest part of the wheat berry, and is essential for new growth. If not properly stored, the oil in wheat germ will get rancid, which makes the grain unfit. Use wheat germ immediately after purchase or freeze. See Chapter 6—Tasty Toppings.

	Calories	Carbohydrate	Fat	Protein	Sodium	Fiber
¼-cup	77	10 g	1 g	6 g	0	6 g

Wheat germ—Toasted

	Calories	Carbohydrate	Fat	Protein	Sodium	Fiber
¼-cup	108	12 g	4 g	8 g	trace	4 g

White Flour (see all-purpose flour)
When the wheat germ and wheat bran are removed from the whole-wheat berry, the resulting endosperm is milled to give us wheat flour or otherwise referred to as white flour.

Whole-wheat flour 100%

The 100% whole-wheat flour—endosperm, wheat germ and wheat berry—that is grown today has not changed much over the years. To make Basic dark bread, use 100% whole-wheat flour.

There are three different whole-wheat flours: durum whole wheat, soft whole wheat and hard whole wheat.

Durum whole-wheat flour is high in gluten and has a yellow appearance; it is best for pasta.

Soft whole-wheat flour is low in gluten, and is best for pastries.

Hard whole-wheat flour is high in gluten and is best for bread baking.

	Calories	Carbohydrate	Fat	Protein	Sodium	Fiber
¼-cup	130	26 g	0	5 g	0	4 g

♥ *February 3rd 2000—In the Roman Catholic newspaper "The Monitor", Father John Dietzen answered the question, "What is required, according to law, for bread used in the Eucharist?" Father answered, "The Latin-rite tradition and the present regulations of the Church requires that no ingredients other than wheat flour and water be used in making bread."*

Herbs

Fresh Herbs

Fresh herbs are best used immediately. When baked in bread or frozen in dough, most herbs do not hold their flavor. Experiment.

♦ For unusual flavor and aroma heat fresh herbs with olive oil, and serve as a dip with crusty white bread.

♦ Sprinkle fresh herbs on pizza.

Dried Herbs

Dried herbs are two to three times more intense in flavor than fresh herbs. Whereas fresh herbs are delicious sprinkled on bread, dried herbs are best baked into bread. The baking time and the moisture in the bread releases the good herb flavor and allows it to mingle with the dough. Start with ¼ teaspoon per 4-cups flour.

♦ Experiment with familiar herbs. Mix a few and add to a Basic recipe.

♦ Consider multi-herb bread with oregano, marjoram and rosemary.

Fresh and Dried Herbs

♦ Basil is superb on fresh pizza.

♦ Chives, with its mild onion flavor, makes a tasty spread.

♦ Coriander bakes favorably in Basic sweet-bread.

♦ Dill is mild and is best used fresh in a spread.

♦ Fennel's licorice flavor is tasty in Basic sweet bread.

♦ Garlic is delicious heated with olive oil and Italian spices.

♦ Marjoram is mild and flavorful for pizza or stuffing.

♦ Oregano is hearty and great with warm olive oil and crisp bread.

♦ Parsley is best when used fresh; it is tasty in bread stuffing.

♦ Rosemary blends well on pizza and in bread stuffing.

♦ Saffron will give white rolls a yellow color. Saffron has an unusual quality—go easy.

♦ Sage has a strong flavors. A little sage goes a long way.

♦ Thyme is tasty in bread stuffing.

♦ Watercress is tangy and flavorful in a sandwich.

There is also cumin, celery, chili, curry, and many others to mix into flour, knead into dough or sprinkle onto bread.

Liquids

Bread can be made with beer, coffee, fruit juice, milk, vegetable juice, water or a combination of liquids.

♦ Whereas water/milk will keep Basic white bread white, other liquids add color and are best mixed for dark flour breads.

♦ Juice from vegetables such as spinach or beet is best added to dark flour breads.

♦ Each liquid adds its own flavor, texture and color.

Beer (ale, stout)

When heated with other liquid, beer loses its alcohol content, but retains its flavor. Beer bread stimulates conversation. Substitute 1-cup beer for 1-cup water in Basic recipe.

	Calories	Carbohydrate	Fat	Protein	Sodium	Fiber
¼-cup	36	4 g	0	0	trace	0

Buttermilk
Buttermilk is the residue from butter making. Substitute ½ cup buttermilk for ½-cup milk.

	Calories	Carbohydrate	Fat	Protein	Sodium	Fiber
¼-cup	25	3 g	1 g	2 g	64 mg	0

♦ Buttermilk powder can be purchased for long-term keeping.

♥ *November 7ᵗʰ 2000—My St. Gregory's—class of 1948—grade school friends continue to meet once or twice a year. At a meeting, in Sea Isle City, NJ, the sky looked cloud curdled. Kate noticed the sky and reminded Betty Jane, Cecilia and myself of the song from the forties, "Oh Buttermilk Sky", by Hoagy Carmichael and Jack Brooks.*

(When Cecilia and Frank [who had attended grade school with Ed] had their daughter Kara in October 1961, they asked Ed and myself to be God Parents. By the following February, we were engaged to be married in August.)

Coffee
Combine coffee (liquid or powder) and chocolate with molasses for dark-dark rye or pumpernickel bread.

	Calories	Carbohydrate	Fat	Protein	Sodium	Fiber
¼-cup	trace	trace	trace	trace	trace	0

♥ *March 5ᵗʰ, 1987—I made five loaves no-name bread: 2-cups coffee, 1-cup molasses, ¼ cup vegetable oil, 4-cups water, 2 lbs whole-wheat flour, 2 lbs rye flour, 2-tablespoons salt, 4-pkg yeast. I ran out of flour and used breakfast cereals. Nice.*

♥ *1970s–1980s—Our Medford, NJ ranch-style home was built in 1922 and had a gas stove. Many times during a summer storm, we were hours without electric. On such days my neighbors and their children visited and enjoyed the gas stove, hot coffee, warm bread and neighborly conversation. In the evening, we lit candles, told stories and recalled a time before electricity.*

Cottage Cheese

Cottage cheese is pure milk in solid form that turns to liquid when heated. For bread making, heat cottage cheese with other liquids until 130°. Cottage cheese improves nutrition without altering white or dark-bread flavor. If not well-blended cottage cheese will give white bread a speckled appearance; this does not alter the fine bread flavor. In Basic recipes, substitute 1-cup small curd cottage cheese for milk.

	Calories	Carbohydrate	Fat	Protein	Sodium	Fiber
4% fat small curd						
¼-cup	54	1 g	2 g	7 g	212 mg	0
1% low fat						
¼-cup	41	1 g	0	7 g	300 mg	0

♦ Nutritious Lunch—cottage cheese, apple butter and slices of Basic dark bread.

♥ *1950s—My mother referred to cottage cheese as 'smearcase' and combined it with apple butter, which at the time, I thought quite distasteful, and in later years I found delicious. (The dictionary reads—Also spelled smier-case—schmieren to smear + kase cheese.)*

Fruit Juice

Fruit juice gives additional flavor and color to sweet bread. Substitute ½ cup fruit juice for ½-cup liquid in Basic recipe.
♦ Simmer dried fruit in water then drain, and use fruit water for liquid in bread making.

Milk

Milk gives bread a pure white look, a smooth texture and a soft crust. Use whole milk (3.3% fat)—recommended for Basic bread recipes—low fat (2% fat) or skim milk (no fat). Skim milk has no fat, fewer calories and as much nutrition as whole milk.

Milk is a food and will not absorb the same amount of dry ingredients as water. When substituting whole milk for water in Basic recipe, less flour will be necessary.

In past years when adding milk to the yeast, we had to first scald milk. And often the milk was sour resulting in 'off' tasting bread. Now, for Basic bread recipe, we heat milk with water until the thermometer reaches 130°, and then mix the liquid with the combined dry ingredients. In less then an hour, in an 80° area, dough is ready for baking. There is no longer the worry about 'off' tasting bread.

	Calories	Carbohydrate	Fat	Protein	Sodium	Fiber
Whole 3.3%						
¼-cup	38	3 g	2 g	2 g	30 mg	0
Low fat 2%						
¼-cup	30	3 g	1 g	2 g	31 mg	0
Low fat 1%						
¼-cup	25	3 g	1 g	2 g	31 mg	0
Non-fat						
¼-cup	22	3 g	trace	2 g	31 mg	0

♦ To make bread dairy free, use all water.
♦ For a dark crust, brush dough with a few tablespoons of milk before baking.

♥ *1940s—Before milk was sold homogenized, it was necessary to shake the milk bottle to circulate the cream. During the forties, when homogenized milk became available in the U. S., mothers were vocal in their resistance. The milk had no 'top cream' to use in coffee or on berries.*
When the milkman delivered milk before daybreak—most every home had milk delivered—on a below freezing morning, milk sat on the doorstep and froze. As the liquid expanded it pushed the frozen top-cream up through the cardboard bottle cap. Fresh frozen cream, with its naturally sweet taste was a treat.

Milk Powder

When making bread, add powdered milk with the dry ingredients. Or, add powdered milk to heated liquid and then add to dry ingredients. Use additional powdered milk for extra nutrition—as much as ½ cup powdered milk to 4-cups flour. 5-tablespoons powdered milk = 8-oz reconstituted

Reconstituted non fat milk

	Calories	Carbohydrate	Fat	Protein	Sodium	Fiber
¼-cup	20	3 g	0	2 g	30 mg	0

♥ *Hot chocolate for a crowd-*

Hot chocolate—mix 2 ½-cups (one envelope) powder milk with 4-cups water, 1-cup sugar and ½-cup cocoa powder. This is wonderful warm on below cold-tolerance day. Serve with—what else—home baked Basic white, sweet or dark bread.

Milk—Evaporated

Evaporated milk is whole milk with half the water removed—concentrated milk.

	Calories	Carbohydrate	Fat	Protein	Sodium	Fiber
¼-cup	80	6 g	4 g	4 g	60 mg	0

Milk—Ultra Pasteurized

Ultra pasteurized liquid milk can be stored on the closet shelf for months, and is convenient for bread baking.

	Calories	Carbohydrate	Fat	Protein	Sodium	Fiber
Whole milk						
¼-cup	40	3 g	2 g	2 g	32 mg	0
Low fat						
¼-cup	30	2 g	0 g	2 g	30 mg	0

♥ *1990s—On a cold sunless day, Maureen recommended a soul-warming beverage: skim milk 8 ounces heated, ¼ teaspoon vanilla and pinch nutmeg. (It is now my favorite pick-me-up.)*

Soymilk
Use soymilk in place of whole milk in the Basic bread recipe.

	Calories	Carbohydrate	Fat	Protein	Sodium	Fiber
¼-cup	45	6 g	2 g	3 g	21 mg	0

Vegetable Water
For additional nutrition, use liquid from cooked fruit in sweet-bread recipe, and liquid from cooked vegetables in high-nutrition dark-bread recipes.

Water
Have water close to 130° when adding to dry ingredients.

♦ Diet white bread is made without oil and milk and just water for liquid.
♦ For a crisp crust, before and during baking, brush bread with cold water.
♦ When exhausted, mental energy evaporates and it is impossible to think past the moment. Weariness, most often, can be removed with an eight-ounce glass of water.

♥ *February 22nd 1987—Maureen gave a psychological test to family members, which shows interesting results. We find that the family has various problems but nothing major. I made six loaves dark bread (no salt) and six loaves white bread (water and no milk).*

Nuts
Nuts are high in nutrition, taste and texture. Because nuts have a high fat content, use shortly after purchase or freeze. Add 1-cup nuts, whole, chopped or ground to Basic recipes.

Blanched Nuts
To blanch nuts, cover with water and bring to a boil. Drain and cool. For a nutritious treat, knead 1-cup whole blanched nuts into Basic dark recipe dough.

Toasted Nuts—Roasted Nuts
Preheat oven to 350°. Place nuts on a flat baking sheet and bake for 15 minutes. Sprinkle with sugar or spice and bake for another five minutes: according to size. Basic sweetbread does wonders for 1-cup toasted nuts.

Almonds

Almonds are sold whole, halved, slivered, ground and as a paste. Mix whole or halved almonds into dry ingredients. Knead slivered almonds into Basic sweet-recipe dough. Sprinkle ground almonds onto baked bread. Spread almond paste onto sweet buns. Almond paste is a simple pleasure on holiday bread.

	Calories	Carbohydrate	Fat	Protein	Sodium	Fiber
¼-cup slivered	190	5 g	15 g	6 g	0 mg	4 g

♦ Cover holiday bread with icing, slivered almonds and colorful glazed fruit.
♦ Mix ½ cup slivered almonds with ½ cup coconut and knead into Basic dark dough. Bake and enjoy

♥ *1963—While living in England, I ordered a cake for Edward's Baptismal Celebration, the cake was covered with marzipan: a delicious mixture of almond paste, sugar and egg whites.*

Coconut

Coconut is sold sweet or unsweetened, and coconut is sold as whole nut, in strands, chips, flakes and granulated. Knead 1-cup sweet or unsweetened coconut into Basic white, sweet or dark dough.

Coconut—dried and sweetened

	Calories	Carbohydrate	Fat	Protein	Sodium	Fiber
¼-cup	117	11	8	1	61	1 g

♦ For a sweet sensation, sprinkle coconut with grated orange, lemon or lime peel onto sweet bread or icing.

Hazelnuts

Beside the additional taste and texture, ground hazelnuts give a speckled look to Basic bread. Unusual.
Add 1-cup to Basic recipe, or sprinkle ¼-cup ground hazel nuts onto icing.

	Calories	Carbohydrate	Fat	Protein	Sodium	Fiber
¼-cup	200	6 g	18 g	4 g	0	4

Pecans

Pecans are a sweet tasting and decorative addition when placed atop holiday sweet bread icing.

♥Pecans are at their best when sampled from atop Ethel's Philadelphia Cinnamon buns.

	Calories	Carbohydrate	Fat	Protein	Sodium	Fiber
¼-cup	210	4 g	22 g	3 g	0	3 g

Walnuts

Walnuts are good in bread and on bread: whole, chopped or ground. Knead ½-cup chopped walnuts into Basic dough.

	Calories	Carbohydrate	Fat	Protein	Sodium	Fiber
¼-cup	200	4 g	20 g	5 g	0 mg	2 g

♥ *1969—A family friend, Jerry, placed two walnuts together in one hand and cracked—one walnut against the other to release the nutmeat. My pre school children were in awe at this accomplishment.*

Organic Ingredients

Many manufacturers state that their products are organically grown and processed in accordance to a state's Organic Food Act. Use organic grown or regular field grown ingredients with flavorful success. Home baked bread is simple food with natural ingredients.

Salt

Salt gives flavor and preserves. Too much salt will deter yeast growth. Consider 2-teaspoons salt to 4-cups flour. The salts for bread baking are table salt, celery, coarse and garlic. See Salt in Chapter 7

	Calories	Carbohydrate	Fat	Protein	Sodium	Fiber
1-teaspoon	0	0	0	0	2,300 mg	0

♦Before baking, top bread sticks or rolls with egg white and sprinkle on coarse large salt.
♦To enhance the flavor of breads made without salt, use herbs, extracts and toppings.

♥*January 11ᵗʰ 1987—Lesson learned: When following Basic bread recipe, first place ingredients on counter then replace ingredients as used. I made Basic white bread and omitted the salt. The bread tasted somewhat acceptable with grape jelly.*

Seeds

Seeds such as anise, caraway, flax, poppy and sesame are high in fiber and protein. They are also high in fat and should be stored in the freezer. For texture and flavor, add seeds to Basic bread ingredients after the liquid has cooled. If added with hot liquid, seeds will soften. Seeds are wholesome nutrition, convenient and have great flavor. Experiment.

◆ Anise seed gives bread a sweet licorice flavor. Sprinkle it on sweet toast or add to icing.

◆ Caraway seeds enhance rye flavor, and are great in pumpernickel bread.

◆ Flax seed is wildly different in dark bread—knead ½-cup flaxseed into dark flour dough.

◆ Poppy seed—sprinkle poppy seed on white, sweet or dark rolls.

◆ Sesame seeds are mild tasting, and are at their best on Basic white rolls.

To keep seeds from popping from bread while baking, brush dough with egg white and then sprinkle on seeds.

◆ Consider multi seed bread. To Basic recipe, add 1-tablespoon each: caraway, flax, poppy and sesame seed.

♥*1975—Maureen brought an Irish scone to her 5ᵗʰ grade class for an ethnic food party. Weeks later her teacher, David Ainsworth, commented to me about the delicious Irish scone, and could he have the family recipe. He was disappointed to hear that the original recipe (without anise seeds) came from "The Family Circle" magazine and not from Maureen's Irish grandparents.*

♥*March 5ᵗʰ 1994—I used 1.7 oz jar caraway seed in five-loaf recipe that included whole wheat and rye flour. Good flavor.*

Spice

Spices add a flavorful change to Basic white, sweet and dark bread. A spice should enhance all ingredients and not stand alone in taste. Dark flours have their own hearty flavor, and quite a bit more spice is necessary. Since the spice shelf life is about one year, mark the container with date of purchase.

Suggested Spice
Allspice, Apple Pie, Cinnamon, Cloves, Coriander, Garlic, Ginger, Mustard, Nutmeg, Poultry, Pumpkin Pie, Pepper, Saffron, Salt

♥ *Early 1980s—My neighbor Hattie enjoys cooking. She told me, "I'm tired of reading recipes that call for spices that are never in my closet, or too costly to use only once and then watch the spice grow old in the closet."*

Sweeteners
Sweeteners for bread baking are, brown sugar, confectioner's sugar, honey, granulated sugar, maple sugar, molasses and powder sugar.

♦ Heat liquid sweeteners—brown sugar too—along with milk and water.
♦ Basic dark dough interchanges with all sweeteners including molasses.
♦ When baking sweet bread, watch the baking time and temperature—sweet breads brown fast.

Brown Sugar
Light/dark brown sugar is sugar cane with more/less molasses extracted. In Basic dark recipe, substitute equal amounts brown sugar for white sugar. Dissolve brown sugar with recipe required warm liquid before adding to dry ingredients. Use light or dark brown sugar to top sweet buns.

	Calories	Carbohydrate	Fat	Protein	Sodium	Fiber
¼-cup	136	36 g	0	0	0	0

♦ Sprinkle 1-tablespoon brown sugar with 1-tablespoon butter on bread, and place under broiler until the sweet butter melts into the brown sugar, or the brown sugar melts into the sweet butter. Um!

Corn Syrup

Dark or light corn syrup is a liquid sweetener that is made from corn and blends well with other sweeteners. Unless you prefer a very dark sugar topping, use light corn syrup for Ethel's Sticky Cinnamon buns. Use dark corn syrup to top French toast.

Corn syrup—light or dark

	Calories	Carbohydrate	Fat	Protein	Sodium	Fiber
¼-cup	240	60 g	0	0	70 mg	0

♦ 1-cup-granulated sugar mixed with ¼ cup water will equal 1-cup light corn syrup.

♥ *1940s—Corn syrup was immediately available as a sugar substitute during WW11.*

Confectioners' Sugar

Confectioners' sugar is an extra fine powder sugar. See Powder Sugar.

♥ *Early in 1970s—I particularly remember one Boy Scout meeting while living in Sterling Park, VA when, as scout leader assistant for Edwards troop, I helped to teach the boys to make bread. The lesson learned was to have bread baked in advance and in abundance for snacking.*

♥ *Mid 1970s—At one point, during my children's growing years, there was a child in each branch of the scouts: Anna/Brownies, Daniel/Cub Scouts, Maureen/Girl Scouts and Edward/Boy Scouts. I too was involved as leader and as baker of sweet bread snacks.*

Granulated Sugar

Sugar beet is from white beets grown in temperate or cold climates. Sugar cane is a tropical, or subtropical grass and is slightly sweeter than sugar beet. Either sugar beet or sugar cane can be refined for granulated table sugar.

For tangy sweet flavor, mix granulated sugar with grated lemon or orange zest. Or mix with cinnamon, anise seed, or vanilla extract and sprinkle on warm Basic sweet bread.

	Calories	Carbohydrate	fat	Protein	Sodium	Fiber
¼-cup	192	48 g	0	0	0	0

♥ *Mid 1960s—When I started to make bread, my mother-in-law Mary shared her childhood bread memories with me. She remembered that her mother, Mame, mixed and kneaded bread ingredients on the kitchen table, every Tuesday. Mary said, "When I came home from school, I knew from the aroma that it was bread-baking day." Mary often reminisced about her mother's raisin bread with sugar-glaze topping.*

♥ *In 1984—On visits to bakeries in Munich, Germany I was tempted by cream filled, icing topped, chocolate-covered pastries. Moreover, in Germany one could view the goodies, purchase a portion to enjoy, and then sit at a table with coffee and the provided newspaper. Nice. Although tasty, the pastry had something missing. Germany uses sugar beets, and U. S. uses a naturally sweeter sugar—sugar cane. There was a distinct difference in sweetness—such a 'caloric' time I had researching this problem.*

Honey

Honey is a sticky sweet, produced from pollen in the honey sack of the bee. It is stored in double layers of hexagonal cells made from beeswax. Its flavor depends on the bee's food source. It is a natural sweetener, and sweeter than white sugar. When following Basic sweet bread recipe, replace granulated sugar with honey by heating with the liquid ingredients.

	Calories	Carbohydrate	Fat	Protein	Sodium	Fiber
¼-cup	256	68	0	0	4 mg	0

♦ Serve honey on bread, buns or French toast.
♦ Raisin bread sandwiched with honey is a dessert.

♥ *1990s—Because Ed enjoys fly-fishing for trout, we—as a family—most often camped in the Northern states. And for many years we camped in a 'pop-up camper'. Now we have a camper with heat/AC, a flush toilet and an oven (I could bake bread), which we keep at Mountain Creek Campground in Gardners, PA. We miss sleeping in a tent: the stars, the moonlight and the middle of-the-night family walk to the rest rooms.*

Molasses

Molasses is the sediment when sugar cane or beet sugar is processed for table sugar. Grandmother used molasses in home remedies. When used in bread baking, molasses has a distinct taste. For dark and delicious bread substitute molasses for white sugar and add 2-tablespoons grated orange peel.

	Calories	Carbohydrate	Fat	Protein	Sodium	Fiber
¼-cup	188	48 g	0	0	44 mg	0

♥ *January 1ˢᵗ 1996—An article in The Philadelphia Inquirer by Rick Nichols on Molasses stated, "Alas for the masses who don't use molasses".*

Powder Sugar

Powder sugar is a fine grade cane sugar that has been pulverized and mixed with cornstarch. It blends readily for icing. It is also referred to as confectioners' sugar.

	Calories	Carbohydrate	Fat	Protein	Sodium	Fiber
¼-cup	124	32 g	0	0	0	0

♦ Mix 1-cup powder sugar, 1-teaspoon vanilla extract, 2-tablespoons milk, and 1-tablespoon butter and cover raisin bread or buns.

Splenda®

Splenda is a no-calorie sweetener that works quite well in bread making.

	Calories	Carbohydrate	Fat	Protein	Sodium	Fiber
¼-cup	0	4 g	0	0	0	0

White Sugar (See Granulated Sugar)

Yeast
For higher, fluffier bread add additional 1-teaspoon yeast to Basic recipe.
For additional yeast information refer to Yeast in Chapter 4—Mix, Knead, Bake and Serve.

	Calories	Carbohydrate	Fat	Protein	Sodium	Fiber
1-Package	20	3 g	trace	3 g	4 mg	0

♦ Yeast will keep in cool dry place for months and in the freezer for a year.
♦ Yeast is sold in ¼ oz packets. Use one packet for one-loaf recipe and 4-yeast packets for five-loaf recipe.
♦ When following the five-loaf recipe, use 4 yeast packets. Experience has shown me that if 5-yeast packets are used in Basic five-loaf bread recipe, the bread is far too light and airy.
♦ Purchase dry yeast in 1-pound vacuum packed jar or individual ¼ oz packages—2¼-teaspoon dry yeast = ¼ oz packet.
♦ One package—¼-oz—dry yeast = one cake—0.6-oz—compressed yeast

♥ *November 21ˢᵗ 1993—I used yeast packets that had expired two months prior. I had mixed the dry ingredients before recognizing the date. Although it is not a good idea to use expired yeast, I went ahead and kneaded etc. The bread looked great and had the same delicious outcome.*

Bread ingredients are Natural Foods

6

Tasty Toppings and Wholesome Meals

Tasty Toppings

Tasty Toppings in this chapter: Apple Butter, Apple Cider, Apple Sauce, Blueberry Elegance, Bread Crumbs, Brown Sugar, Cinnamon, Coconut, Cranberry, Cream Cheese, Extracts/Food Coloring, Fruit Fresh/Dry Fruit, Glaze, Granola, Herbs, Honey, Icing, Jam, Jelly, Mame's Warm Sugar Glaze, Maple Sugar, Maple Syrup, Marmalade, Nutmeg, Nuts, Peaches, Pizza, Powder Sugar, Salt, Spice, Strawberries, Streusel, Sugar and Toasted Wheat Germ

Tasty Toppings
For the most part home baked bread needs no topping. But there are occasions when it might seem shabby to serve—just bread. On such occasions consider bread with butter. If per chance, something more is required then try a sweet or savory topping.

Knead tasty toppings into dough or sprinkle onto flattened dough. Drizzle tasty toppings onto just baked bread or sprinkle on day old slices. Serve tasty topping (cinnamon/sugar, jam and jelly) in odd-shape dishes. Serve honey in a pitcher: honey is a sticky-mess but worth it. Some foods such as warm applesauce, fresh peaches and sugared strawberries are more pleasurable when served with home-baked bread.

♥ *1960s–2000s—In my kitchen closet, refrigerator and freezer there are ingredients: sugar, spice, fruit, nuts etc. that can be added to dough or to bread. I am like a kid in the candy shop deciding.*

Apple Butter

The home takes on an appetizing aroma while apples and spices simmer. To make apple butter, allow nine hours: apple cider, apples and spice.

For slow even cooking use a crock-pot.

For good-tasting nutrition, serve Basic dark bread with apple butter.

Stove top/apple butter—all day low simmer

Mix 1-quart apple cider with 10-large skinned and chopped apples—simmer 4 hours.

Add 2-cups brown sugar—simmer 4 hours.

Add 1-teaspoon each, cinnamon, cloves, all spice.

Simmer ½-hour longer or until reduced to desired consistency.

Stirring and taste testing ensures proper consistency.

Microwave oven/apple butter

Mix 1-quart apple cider with 10-large skinned and chopped apples.

Cook 1 ½-hrs in the microwave oven.

Add 2-cups brown sugar and cook one hour longer.

Add 1-teaspoon each—cinnamon, cloves and all spice and cook another ½-hour.

To insure good consistency, taste often.

♥ *October 12*[th] *1979—During Medford, NJ yearly fall festival, apples simmer throughout the day and apple-spice aroma is a magnet to the event. I wanted to make apple bread, and use apple cider for liquid, but the apple cider disappeared before I got around to making bread.*

♥ *November 12*[th]*, 1993—I made apple butter in the microwave: delicious tasting, granular yet smooth. As with homemade bread, homemade apple butter does not have as fine a texture as supermarket.*

Apple Cider

Heat apple cider, add cinnamon stick, and serve at brunch with fruit, cheese and Basic dark bread.

♥ *1970s—From the ground below the crab apple tree, Edward, Dan and their friends quietly collected crab apples. And then went to war with each other.*

Applesauce

For delicious applesauce, cook 12 whole cooking apples—skin and core—with 1-cup water in a covered pot for 30 minutes. Press the cooked apples through a heavy strainer then add sugar to taste.

♥ *1970s—We picked apples at Larchmont farm, and enjoyed applesauce, apple pie and apple cake. Although we enjoyed picking apples, just as important were the cinnamon doughnuts and apple cider that were sold at the farm.*

Aunt Rachel's chunky applesauce

For chunky applesauce, skin and slice 12 tart cooking apples into eighths, add 3/4-cup water, cover and cook on medium heat for 20 minutes or until tender—add sugar to taste.

♥ *1970s—After the children were served chunky applesauce at Aunt Rachel's house, my applesauce recipe lost first place.*

Blueberry Elegance

Mix ½-cup sugar with 2-teaspoons cornstarch, stir in ½-cup water, and add 1-pint blue berries. Simmer five minutes. Use blueberry elegance as topping for bread or bread pudding.

♥ *1970s–1980s—At a farm deep in the Pine Barrens, We picked blueberries and placed them into a three-pound coffee can. A rope long enough to loop around our neck and through holes in the can, held the can waist high. While we laughed and picked berries on one side of the berry bushes, we could hear families discussing berry abundance and good flavor on the other side. We dropped a berry handful into the can and two berry handfuls into our mouth. When we finished picking, we weighed the berries, and paid per pound. The berries were placed into plastic bags for travel home.*
At home, we enjoyed blueberry sauce, blueberry shortcake and blueberry pancakes. We froze whole berries for the winter, and before summer's end, we found that frozen blue berries tasted delicious.

♥ *After my mother-in-law berry picked with the children, she commented, "Since we ate so many berries while on the field, it is a good thing that we're not weighed on our way to and from the field."*

Berries Frozen

To fast-freeze blueberries or strawberries—first wash and pat dry on paper towel. Next place on cookie sheet and freeze for few hours. Finally remove from freezer, place berries into freezer bag and back into freezer.

Bread Crumbs

Use Basic sweet breadcrumbs under or over vanilla pudding or between chocolate and vanilla pudding layers. See Below—Wholesome meals/Bread Crumb Recipe.

Brown Sugar Sweetness

For brown sugar sweetness, blend ½-cup brown sugar, ½-cup soft butter, ½-cup flour, and 1-teaspoon cinnamon together with a fork, and top Basic dough. Or sprinkle brown sugar sweetness on just baked buns, or top sliced bread and place under the broiler for a few minutes.

♥ *June 1993—On a vacation in Western Pennsylvania, we visited a restaurant at a turnpike exit near Somerset, PA. We could view the baker adding cinnamon and sugar to kneaded dough. The waitress served a small basket with two large cinnamon buns—warm—with icing. An unexpected delight.*

Cinnamon/Sugar

Mix 1-tablespoon cinnamon with ¼ cup sugar, and sprinkle this mixture between layers of Basic sweet dough or top warm buttered toast.

♥ *1974/75—As a family we enjoyed hockey: Bobby Clark and Stanley Cup Season.—"Let's Go Flyers"—and hot buttered Cinnamon bread.*

Coconut, Toasted

Toast 1-cup coconut by placing on a baking sheet and setting under broiler. Watch closely.
For a surprise sweet bun, place toasted coconut atop powder sugar icing. (See icing/powder sugar below.)

Cranberry Sauce

For whole cranberry sauce mix 4-cups cranberries, 1-cup sugar, and 1-cup water—gently boil 20 minutes—cool and refrigerate or freeze.

For cranberry jelly mix 4-cups cranberries, 1-cup water—gently boil 15 minutes—strain, and discard skins. Add 1-cup sugar and boil 5 minutes. Cranberries are the perfect bread-stuffing complement. (See Stuffing.)

♥ *December 25th*—*Our Christmas meal includes whole fresh cranberry sauce—tart and tasty and the sweeter canned cranberry sauce, which many children and adults prefer. A turkey sandwich made with home baked white bread and served with tart and tasty cranberry sauce is an after-holiday favorite.*

Cream Cheese and Pineapple
Mix 1-cup cream cheese with ¼-cup well-drained crushed pineapple. Pineapple cream cheese makes a delightful lunch when sandwiched between Basic dark bread.

Cream Cheese Icing
When looking for a different flavor to top fruit bread, substitute cream cheese for butter in icing recipes—1-cup powder sugar, 2-tablespoons cream cheese, 1½-tablespoons milk.

♥ *1984*—*In Munich, Germany, I enjoyed pretzels for breakfast. They were cut length way, toasted and covered with Kraft® Philadelphia cream cheese.*

♥ *1990s–2000s*—*With every visit to Grandmom's and Grandpop's house, Emma, Madeleine and Rebecca request white bread—toasted or not—covered with butter or cream cheese.*

Extracts and Food coloring
Enhance bread or icing with extracts—vanilla, almond, lemon etc. or with a food coloring—red, blue, yellow.

Fresh Fruit
Mix 1-pint blueberries, raspberries or strawberries with 1-tablespoon sugar. Mash fruit, and serve over thick bread slice—include a spoon and a bib.

♥ *1970s–1980s*—*For my children, the picking season in Burlington County, NJ began in June with Strawberries, July/blueberries, August/peaches and September/ apples. Although we never picked corn, or tomatoes we certainly ate our share of NJ corn on or off the cob and NJ tomatoes sliced or in a sauce.*

Fruit—Dry
Puree dry fruit with honey and top fresh baked buns or serve on Basic sweet toast.

Fruit Zest—Lemon/lime/orange
Grated lemon, lime or orange zest—thin peel—makes a refreshing icing. Do not use the bitter tasting white that lies just under the colorful zest. The oil in lemon, lime and orange zest adds tantalizing taste and color to bread and to icing. Grate 1-tablespoon colorful zest into ¼-cup white sugar, and sprinkle on warm sweet bread.
For a refreshing change knead 2-tablespoon of orange, lemon or lime zest into dough or grate onto icing.

Glaze—Jelly or Jam
Warm store purchased jelly or jam and top just bake bread or buns. For proper glaze consistency, add 1-tablespoon water to 1-cup jelly.

Glaze—Sugar
For sugar glaze mix ¾-cup powder sugar with 1-tablespoon water or milk.

Glaze—Mame's warm sugar glaze
Mix 1-tablespoons hot water and ¼-cup granulated sugar.
Stir to dissolve and sprinkle on just baked sweet bread or buns.

Granola
Enjoy granola with yogurt for breakfast, sandwiched between buttered bread for lunch and by the handful for snack—a sweet-tooth delight.

Granola is a mixture that includes favorite bread ingredients: bran, oats, wheat germ, toasted wheat germ, almonds, walnuts, hazelnuts, sesame seeds, raisins, cranberries, apricots, honey etc.

Toasted whole-wheat germ will burn—lesson learned. Add toasted whole wheat germ with, fruit and honey, the ingredients that do not require baking.

Granola Recipe
First, in a large roasting pan mix 2-cups oats, 2-cups nuts and 1-cup wheat germ.
Next, bake at 350° for 10 minutes, then stir the mixture and bake for 10 additional minutes.

After mixture is baked, blend in 1-cup dry fruit (dates, apples, apricots or raisins), 1-cup toasted wheat germ, 1-cup mixed seeds and 1-teaspoon vanilla.
Finally add ½-cup honey, which is the glue that holds the mixture together. Use within the next few weeks or freeze in small bags

Add a full cup of honey to granola, and perhaps you too will find the mixture too, too tasty.

I have been known to use the broiler for fast toasting granola ingredients, but if distracted—for seconds—the ingredients burn. As the saying goes, "Haste makes waste". It is best to slow toast mixture in the oven.

♥*Early 1970s—Ed and I were hardly awake when the children presented a Mother's day gift—a box of granola. As a family, we talked and immediately finished the granola.*

Herb Dip—Recipe
Herb dips are best when made with fresh herbs.

Fresh herbs with butter-
Mix ½-cup soft butter with 1-tablespoon fresh herbs: parsley, rosemary, thyme, oregano, tarragon and/or etc. Serve warm for dipping or refrigerate and serve as spread.

Fresh herbs with olive oil-
Mix ½-cup olive oil, 1-tablespoon fresh herbs and clove-crushed garlic.
Or, substitute 1 teaspoon dried herbs. Heat and serve with white hard crusted bread.

Honey topping
Place ½ cup honey into 9" baking pan, top with Basic sweet dough slices—bake.
Or, butter toast and drizzle with honey—the absolute best.
Let pecans set for a few days in a cup of honey. Serve with Basic dark bread.

Icing
Icing is the difference between simple and elegant.
Mix 1-cup powder sugar, 2-tablespoons soft butter and 1½-tablespoons milk.
Blend all together until smooth. Add ½-teaspoon flavor or drop of food color.
Or for a gooey glaze, blend 2-tablespoon milk with 1-cup powder sugar.

Icing/butter
A favorite icing is white bread covered—crust-to-crust—with cold butter.
Another favorite icing is sweet-buns brushed with melted butter and sprinkled with granulated sugar.

Icing celebrations
Add addition color, crunch and flavor to icing
½-teaspoon almond extract with a few almonds
½-teaspoon lemon extract with coconut
2-tablespoons lemon/lime/orange juice to 1-cup powder sugar
1-tablespoon grated lemon, orange or lime rind
Use the colorful zest, and not the bitter white under skin.
½-teaspoon maple extract with a few pecans
½-teaspoon nutmeg with ground walnuts
½-teaspoon cinnamon with granola

♥ *July 4th 1963—In Yorkshire, England, I prepared a cake to celebrate my fun-time holiday—the 4th of July. While covering the cake with red/white/blue icing, my English neighbor unexpectedly visited. Her comment, "You are living in the country that lost the war: this is not a day to celebrate."*

Jam or Jelly (see Glaze)
When making jam or jelly, mix ¾ cup sugar with 1-cup of fruit, and heat until sugar melts—refrigerate or freeze. A first class conveyer for jam or jelly is home-baked bread.

Jam is cooked for short time or not cooked at all, and includes the fruit bits. If necessary, sugar can be added.
Jelly is cooked longer, strained to eliminate the fruit bits and then sugar is added if necessary.
Look to Sure Jell®, a product that helps jell jelly. If, like myself, you cannot imagine straining the good fruit and throwing away the fruit bits, make jam.

♥ *Mid 1990s—While in Charlotte, I was at breakfast with Rachel who said, "Do it myself." The two-year old put grape jelly on her bread, and placed the bread upside down onto her extended tongue. The ensuing smile showed that the grape jelly made fast contact with her taste buds, her mouth, her chin and the table. The eyes told the story.*

Maple Sugar

Maple sugar is sweet, sweet enjoyment. Sprinkled on just-baked Basic dark bread and place under broiler.

Maple Syrup

Grate the rind from an orange into 1-cup maple syrup, heat mixture and top sweet buns.

Marmalade

Marmalade is the rind and juice from lemon, orange or grapefruit cooked with sugar. The flavor carries a delicious tang. Make or purchase marmalade and top Basic dark bread.

♥ *1963—I made marmalade with thick-skin oranges from Seville, Spain, and it was delicious. But the sugar to fruit composition was staggering—2 pounds oranges to 5 pounds sugar. When I purchase a small jar of marmalade, I am not as aware of this composition.*

Nutmeg

For tasty bread topping, mix a pinch nutmeg with cinnamon/sugar recipe.

Nuts

Home baked bread does wonders for nuts: ground, chopped or whole. Butter a bread slice and sprinkle on ground nuts then top with another buttered bread slice: good nutrition, good flavor and good fun.

Nut Butters

For nut butters follow blender directions. Spread ½-cup on flattened dough before baking, or lather nut butters on warm buns. For a lunchtime treat, spread 2-tablespoons nut butter on thick slice dark flour bread and place under the broiler. Watch closely.

Peaches

For a summer afternoon treat, sweeten sliced fresh peaches, and serve with buttered sweet raisin bread. Five nice size peaches equals two cups sliced. To remove peach skin, plunge peach into boiling water for a few seconds. (This also works for tomatoes.) There is absolutely no comparison between sliced fresh peach and sliced canned peaches. What takes place from field, to cannery to store shelf?

Somewhere the good peach freshness is lost. Peaches are delicious—straight from the tree, sliced and served cold with few sprinkles granulated sugar or heated and sprinkled with brown sugar. Grilled peaches make for mealtime conversation.

♥ *1970s–1990s—During the peach season, we picked—ate—peaches that hung heavy from trees, and we placed them into baskets for ease in transporting home. On summer afternoons, peaches were cool, sweet and juicy.*

Pizza Toppings
Cheese and olive oil—Brush dough with olive oil and sprinkle with cheese
Cheese—Ricotta, mozzarella, Parmesan
Spinach—Chop fresh spinach, or thaw and drain frozen spinach
(Use paper towels to squeeze water from frozen spinach.)
Combine the spinach with grated cheese and Italian spice, and sprinkle on the dough.
This pizza is extra special when topped with a few dabs of ricotta cheese.
Consider—herbs/
hot peppers/
mushrooms—fresh or marinated/
olives—black or green/
onions—raw or steamed/
peppers—green or yellow/
pineapple chunks/
spices—basil or rosemary/
tomatoes—fresh or roasted
Slice small canned tomatoes but do not use liquid in the can.
Too much liquid will make the dough soggy.

Serve pizza warm pizza for breakfast. Ask any teenager about this fine breakfast.

♥ *1987—While visiting Montana for our 25ᵗʰ wedding-anniversary holiday, we were introduced to pizza topped with pineapple chunks, tomato slices and cheese grated. This sweet and savory pizza was a shock to our taste buds, yet others enjoyed the difference.*

♥ *Early 1990s—While visiting with cousin Marjorie and her husband Wilson in Charlotte, NC, their daughter, Stacy, served crusty pizza with fruit toppings for breakfast.*

♥ *1998—Before Anna purchased her home, she invited Ed and myself to meet her at the house. When I told Maureen that we were going to look at Anna's new house, Maureen told her sister-in-law Patty. The real-estate agent and Anna were shocked to find nine family members wishing to check out the house. Of course, we were not short on opinions. After our walk through the house, we went for Pizza and laughs. We repeated this process for a few houses until Anna (and all) agreed on the perfect Anna house.*

Powder Sugar
Powder sugar is an elegant topping when sprinkled from a sugar shaker onto sweet buns.

Salt
Salt—celery, garlic and/or herb salt—can be mixed with warm water and brushed on crusty bread while baking. Sprinkled coarse salt on pretzels or bread sticks.

Spice
What spice do you enjoy? Mix ¼-cup sugar with 1-tablespoon cinnamon, or with 1-teaspoon nutmeg, or with ¼-teaspoon all spice—try apple pie spice. Each spice has its own hardiness. Experiment.

Strawberries
For strawberry goodness, boil ½ cup water with 1-cup sugar, and then add 1-qt Strawberries, cook a few minutes or until strawberries are just soft.

♥ *1970s–1980s—For strawberry picking we climbed onto the Conte Farm flattop truck, which transported us to the strawberry field. We crawled on the ground to pick strawberries that grew on plants close to the ground. We knew strawberries had to be firm enough to be packed with other strawberries in the provided cardboard container. And, we knew that strawberries once picked would get no riper. We picked the juiciest. And if a strawberry looked extra succulent, we ate it. On the trip home we laughed at our strawberry pink mouth, hands and knees.*

Streusel
Streusel is delicious when baked atop the dough, and delicious on baked buns. Mix—¼-cup melted butter, 1-cup Basic sweet-breadcrumbs, ½-cup chopped nuts—almonds, pecans or walnuts, 1/3-cup white or brown sugar, 1-teaspoon cinnamon- And sprinkle on baked buns. Set under broiler for few minutes: watch closely.

Sugar
White granulated sugar has little flavor. Brown sugar is delicious. Powder sugar is tasty. And flavored sugars are a pleasant surprise. Flavor white granulated sugar with vanilla, nutmeg, cinnamon or lemon/lime zest.

Consider
White sugar—flavored with vanilla on warm sweet buns
Brown sugar—broiled atop buttered white bread
Powder sugar—sprinkled on French toast
Flavored sugar—on holiday breads

Toasted Wheat Germ
Along with high nutrition, toasted wheat germ gives Basic dark bread hearty flavor and a nutty texture. Substitute ½ cup wheat germ to Basic white or dark recipe. Knead ½ cup wheat germ into dough. Sprinkle 1-tablespoon toasted wheat germ on hot buttered toast.

Home baked bread gives sweet memories and lasting round of applause

Wholesome Meals

Whole Loaf, Sliced Bread, Bread Cubed and Bread Crumbs

Wholesome Meals in this chapter
Whole Loaf: Decorating a Loaf, Hippie Dipping, Spinach Dip, Loaf of Fun and Meal in a Loaf,
Sliced Bread: Cookie Cutter Sandwich, Dried Beef, Egg in Toast, French Toast, Honey Toast, Melba Toast, Milk Toast, Round Sandwich, Sandwich Maker, Sandwich Suggestions, Club Sandwich,
Grilled Sandwich, Scarborough Toast and Welsh Rarebit
Bread Cubed: Croutons, Bread Pudding, Kugle, Fondue, Soup, and Stuffing
Crumbed Bread: Breadcrumb Recipe, Topping, Vegetable, Seasoned and Soup

Energize breakfast, lunch, dinner, snack, picnic, and potluck with Basic breads: Whole, Sliced, Cubed and Crumbed. Homemade efforts are appreciated when bread is served hot or cold, toasted or plain, fresh or day old.

Home baked bread, for wholesome meals, can be one to six days old, and home baked bread for wholesome meals can be bread that has been frozen, but home baked bread for wholesome meals cannot be stale bread. Stale bread is bread that is over one week old. Stale bread does not have good flavor, and if used in bread recipe, will make food that tastes stale. See Storage in Chapter 4.

This does not apply to store purchased breads, which have artificial preservatives that keep bread soft and moist for weeks—even months.

Whole Loaf
Use the whole loaf as a table decoration—in a basket with a colorful napkin.
Display the whole loaf as a container for a favorite party dip or salad.
Serve whole bread loaf with a serrated knife for slicing.

Decorating A Dry Loaf
Decorate your mealtime table with bread-in-a-basket. To dry bread, place baked loaf on a rack where air can circulate, and allow bread to dry for two weeks. When dry spray on shellac (optional); a decorative loaf will last for years.

♥ *1976—A well-raised braided-bread loaf had been set to dry then sprayed with shel-lac. The finished product, a light gloss-golden loaf, was placed in a basket with a col-orful napkin and used for months as a kitchen table decoration.*
Dan borrowed the magnificent braided loaf for a class project.
When the project was completed, he refused to tell the teacher that his mother wished stale bread returned.

Hippie Dipping

Utensils—sharp knife, serving dish
Ingredients—one round bread loaf—white or dark, spinach dip (see recipe below)

1—Cut away the top of loaf and remove inner bread.
2—When ready to serve, fill the hollow loaf with spinach dip.
3—Pull apart inner bread and set around loaf for dipping.
4—Replace top crust.

♥ *Mid 1960s—A coworker invited Ed to attend a Philadelphia neighborhood block party. This was a 'hippie' party and we were unmistakably dressed quaint. Our host made us comfortable with food and beverage and neighbors shared original recipes.*
A particular recipe for marijuana cookies caught my attention. Another recipe was for a hollowed out loaf of dark bread filled with grass salad: fresh cut grass mixed with chives, scallion, vinegar and oil.

Spinach Dip

Utensils—mixing bowl, spoon, paper towel
Ingredients—9-oz frozen chopped spinach, 1 package dry vegetable soup mix, 1-pt sour cream

1—Thaw frozen chopped spinach and squeeze water out using paper towels. Do not cook spinach.
2—Mix spinach and sour cream.
3—Add vegetable soup mix, and blend together.
4—Refrigerate for 1 hour before serving.
Fill hollowed out loaf with dip. (See Hippie Dipping above.)

♥ *2000s—Hollowed out pumpernickel bread filled with spinach dip is Anna's party specialty.*

Loaf of Fun

Utensils—sharp knife, serving dish

Ingredients—sliced loaf Basic white, sweet or dark bread, honey, butter, cinnamon, sugar

1—Lather a slice with butter and honey.
2—Cover a slice with butter, cinnamon/sugar.
3—Smear a slice with butter, honey, cinnamon, and sugar.
Repeat with the other slices and reassemble the loaf.
Serve Loaf of Fun for breakfast enjoyment.

Meal in a Loaf

Utensils—long sharp knife, serving dish

Ingredients—loaf white or dark bread, cold filler such as pasta, rice, beans, potato or vegetable salad

1—Remove end slice.
2—Cut away inner loaf while leaving an inch on all sides.
3—Pack filler into loaf—do not have filler too moist.
4—For ease in slicing, refrigerate a few hours before serving.
Use cut-away inner bread for breadcrumbs.

♥ *Mid 1990s—A friend from my social work days enjoyed a loaf of bread for many meals, and sent the following thank-you note:*
What a delicious (and beneficial) surprise! As soon as I hung up my coat, I went for the bread knife!
The texture and delicate sweetness of your bread made it into a mouth-watering main course.
I enjoyed it plain. I enjoyed it with a hint of unsweetened butter. I enjoyed it with a meager wedge of cheese.
Thank you so much for your thoughtfulness. It is sincerely appreciated.
Love, Barb

Bread Sliced

Bread was not sold sliced until the 1930s. Now, sliced bread is served for breakfast, lunch, dinner and snack. And home-baked bread is sliced as narrow as your pinkie or as wide as your thumb. When purchasing bread, the end slices are seldom eaten, but homemade bread 'crust' are the first devoured.

For sandwich enjoyment alternate breads: Basic white, sweet and dark and bread shapes: slices, rolls and buns.

Cookie Cutter Sandwich

Utensils—knife, cookie cutters
Ingredients—full Basic loaf, sandwich spreads such as—cheese and chives, egg salad, peanut butter, fruit spread, ground walnuts, wheat germ, imagination.

1—Remove crust and slice bread length way.
2—Top one slice with sandwich spread and top with another bread slice.
3—Cut bread-sandwich with cookie cutters.
4—Continue with all slices.
Refrigerate for a few hours before serving.
♦ Adults enjoy the mini sandwich convenience.
♦ Children enjoy animal character, cookie cutter fun.
♦ For extra nutrition sprinkle the mini sandwich with toasted wheat germ.
♦ For extra fun sprinkle the animal characters with colorful confetti candies.

Dried Beef

Utensils—knife, measuring cup, frying pan
Ingredients—4-oz butter, 2 to 3-oz dried beef, 4-tablespoons flour, 2-cups milk, 4 slices toasted white bread

1—Melt butter in frying pan.
2—Add dried beef and heat for few minutes.
3—Sprinkle on flour to blend into meat/butter.
4—Slowly add milk—stir well.
5—Cook over medium heat for about 20 minutes or until serving consistency.
6—Serve over toasted home baked white bread.
When you wish to disregard calories, carbohydrates, cholesterol, fat and sodium, make dried beef. It is delicious.

♥ *1940s–2000s—We have been following the same dried beef recipe since the 1940s—my family at Jefferson St. and Ed's family at Rector St. Both families served dried beef over potatoes: mashed, baked or boiled. Ed said, "During the 1950s his mother used canned mushroom soup as liquid."*

Egg in Toast
   Utensils—fry pan, spatula
   Ingredients—egg, butter, bread slice

   1—Heat fry pan and add butter.
   2—Cut an egg size opening in bread.
   3—Put bread slice in fry pan and place egg in cut away area.
   4—Cover pan and cook for a few minutes.
   5—Top with cut away bread and serve.
   This is a wholesome addition to the breakfast menu.

French Toast
   Utensils—fry pan, small dish, fork
   Ingredients—2-slices bread, 2-tablespoons butter, 1-egg fork beaten with ½-cup milk

   1—Fork beat egg/milk
   2—Dip bread into egg mixture.
   3—Heat butter and brown bread on each side.
   Serve this sweetened with maple syrup.
   Use raisin or cinnamon bread for French toast.

♥ *Early 1900s—When my mother was young, fried bread was just that. A slice of bread buttered on both sides, fried and sprinkled with granulated sugar. (In the sixties, while preparing French toast for her grandchildren, my mother reminisced about fried bread.)*

Honey Toast
Blend 1-tablespoon honey with 1-tablespoon soft butter and cover thick slice of toasted home-baked bread.

Melba Toast
Melba toast is thinly sliced bread that is two or three days old and oven toasted—with or without the crust. This toast is great for dieters.
Not dieting—cover with butter or cream cheese.

Milk Toast

Milk toast is bread toasted, buttered lightly then covered with warm milk and sprinkled with granulated sugar.

♥ *Early 1900s—As a child my mother-in-law was served milk toast when she was sick. Her grand mother referred to milk toast as sick toast. The patient felt pampered. (Pampered enough to relate the recipe to her grandchildren during the 1970s.)*

♥ *Bread baking yields tasty, inexpensive memories.*

Sandwich

For lunch, late afternoon or nighttime snack, cover Basic white, sweet or dark bread with high nutrition ingredients. You are the architect. For a sandwich that has something other than ho-hum lunchmeat and mustard, consider these suggestions. And when ready to serve add a garnish: flower or fruit.

Basic white bread: Refried beans & salsa/olives & chopped egg/raisins, nuts & cream cheese/sliced red onion & mayonnaise/watercress & toasted wheat germ

Basic sweet bread: Ground nuts & cream cheese/banana & peanut butter/cream cheese & pineapple/chopped dates & ground nuts/cinnamon, butter & white sugar

Basic dark bread: Blue cheese & black olives/jalapeno peppers & bean salad/ sliced onion & wheat germ/thin apple slices & onion/sharp cheese & mayonnaise
◆ For ease in preparing crust free sandwiches, freeze the loaf then carve away frozen crust.
◆ Keep an ingredient list for mixing and matching.
◆ For sandwich goodness, add 1-tablespoon toasted wheat germ to sandwich filler.
◆ Use yesterday's leftovers with sprouts, garlic, herbs, and horseradish to make a tasty sandwich.
◆ To avoid soggy bread, layer dry lettuce leaf against bread then place moist ingredients between lettuces.
◆ For sandwich crunch, chop vegetables such as asparagus, avocado, broccoli, cabbage, cauliflower, celery, cucumber, onion, pepper, radish, spinach, tomato, zucchini etc.

♥ *Class 1952—While attending West Philadelphia Catholic Girls High School, the popular lunch served in the cafeteria was—potato salad sandwich.*

Sandwich—Club
Utensils—knife, serving dish
Ingredients—three bread slices, ingredients of choice: see sandwich suggestions

1—Cover one bread slice with ingredient of choice.
2—Top ingredients with second bread slice.
3—Cover slice with lettuce, tomato, onion, and pickle.
4—A third bread slice tops the sandwich.
5—Cut into three or four servings and hold together with colorful toothpicks.
This sandwich is best on Basic white or dark bread.
A club sandwich or double-decker sandwich allows your imagination to run wild.
The sandwich should be mouth manageable and not a Dagwood sandwich.

Sandwich—Grilled
Utensils—sandwich maker or fry pan
Ingredients—1-tablespoon butter, 2-slices bread and 3-slices cheese

1—Butter a bread slice.
2—Place cheese on non-buttered side.
3—Cover ingredients with a bread slice.
4—Butter outside slice.
5—Heat a fry pan and brown the bread.
6—Turn and brown on the other side.
The goodness of this sandwich is appreciated noon or nighttime.

Sandwich Maker
Electric sandwich makers toast bread and seal in ingredients. Sandwich makers are fun to use for sweet and savory fillings.

Sandwich—Round
Two favorite bread slices are cut with a round cutter that also removes the crust. Cover slices with cream cheese or peanut butter and sandwich.

♥ *2000s—A round bread cutter removes the crust, and children enjoy a round peanut butter sandwich, which is even tastier when the bread is toasted.*

Scarborough Toast
Utensils—broiler
Ingredients—thick bread slice, butter and brown sugar according to taste

1—Toast thick slice bread on one side.
2—Cover not toasted side with nice amount of butter.
3—Sprinkle with nice amount of brown sugar.
4—Place under broiler until sugar bubbles.
5—Slice bread into three strips and enjoy with a favorite hot beverage.
Pamper yourself—as you would a guest.

♥ *1963—In Scarborough, England, Roundtree's department store served afternoon tea and cinnamon toast with a flourish. The thick bread toast strips were brown and crisp yet warm and soft. Scrumptious. To keep the tea hot, the teapot was covered with a tea cozy. On a bone-chilling day, one was pampered. How nice that there were so many bone-chilling days in Scarborough, England.*

Welsh Rarebit
Utensils—heavy saucepan, mixing bowl
Ingredients—2-cups grated sharp cheese, ¼-cup beer or another liquid, 2-teaspoon mustard, 1-teaspoon Worcestershire sauce, 1-egg/fork-beaten, 4-toasted bread slices, pinch paprika

1—Melt cheese with beer.
2—Add mustard and Worcestershire sauce.
3—Add mixture to fork-beaten egg.
4—Return to pot and stir for few minutes on medium heat.
5—Serve on toast and sprinkle with paprika.
Spice up Welsh rarebit with jalapeno peppers and serve with crisp vegetables.

♥ *1972—We had just moved into our Medford Lakes house, and Ed made and served Welsh rarebit to the family. As a single man Ed was a good cook, and made the meals at his mother's home. But then Ed lost interest in cooking—thus the memory. Fortunately for me, he resumed his cooking interest during the 1990s and now into the 2000s.*

♥ ***October 17th 1949***—*My Aunt Rachel (and my mother) received a letter from The Philadelphia law office of Duane, Morris & Heckscher regarding an inheritance from the British Governments acquisition of minerals from her paternal grandfather's land in Wales. The letter was greeted with great speculation. When the money was received my aunt was heard to say, "It is hardly enough money for a teapot."*

♥ ***February 16th 2002***—*At aunt Rachel's estate sale, I placed a bid on a lovely, gold trimmed, cranberry colored teapot. As I cradled the teapot in my lap, my cousin Margie said, "That's the teapot my mother bought with her 'inheritance money' back in the forties." Marjorie further stated, "If I had known you wanted the teapot, I would have given it to you". But, in fact, I had never seen the teapot before.*

Bread Cubed

Bread cubed can be toasted as for croutons or not toasted as for stuffing. Use Basic white, sweet or dark bread cubes in fondue and pudding, as casserole toppings and for soup or salad. Use bread slices that are 3–4 days old.

If you just dry bread cubes in the oven, bread will be too light. If you brown bread cubes in the broiler, without first drying in the oven, bread will be too soft in the middle. If you do not watch closely, bread will burn. Use a timer.

A meat-less soup, such as split pea, is hearty when topped with bread cubes. Salads such as Caesar and spinach are given the personal touch when topped with bread cubes.

Croutons

Oven—200°
Time—20 minutes + five minutes + two minutes in broiler
Utensils—baking sheet, sharp knife
Ingredients—bread slices that are about three days old—optional—melted butter with herbs

1—Spread thick or thin bread slices—with or without crust—on both sides with melted butter.
2—The butter can be mixed with herbs or spices
(Croutons are tasty without butter.)
3—Cut bread into desired size, and arrange on a baking sheet.
4—Bake 200° for twenty minutes—use a timer.
5—Turn bread and replace in oven for another five minutes.
6—Place under broiler for two minutes. Turn and broil an additional minute.
7—Cool and use immediately or freeze.
Both oven and broiler time are according to bread dryness and size.
Once you enjoy soup or a salad with homemade croutons, you will have a problem purchasing packaged croutons.

♥ *December 1993—A favorite food is Ed's Caesar salad with Basic white-bread croutons. We have a massive wood salad bowl, and when Ed takes this bowl filled with delicious Caesar salad to a party he is immediately famous. This year, we attended a holiday party at our neighbors Joan and John.*

Bread Pudding
Oven—350°
Time—50 minutes
Utensils—baking dish 9" x 13"
Ingredients—5-bread slices 3–4 days old, 2-tablespoons butter cut small, 4-cups milk, 4-eggs, ¼-cup sugar, 1-teaspoon vanilla

1—Cut bread into small cubes.
2—Mix milk, eggs, sugar and vanilla.
3—Place bread in mixture and top with butter.
4—Bake 350° for 50 minutes or until 'set'.
Pudding is 'set' when a knife inserted into center comes away clean.
Serve bread pudding warm for dinnertime dessert or cold for breakfast nutrition. For a hearty pudding, use whole wheat bread, and for a generous pudding, add ½-cup raisins.

Pineapple Kugle—Miriam's
Oven—350°
Time—50–60 minutes
Utensils—baking dish 9" x 13"
Ingredients—½-cup sugar, 2-sticks melted butter, 8-eggs, 2—1 lb cans crushed pineapple with syrup, 10-slices bread—3–4 days old

1—Add sugar to melted butter and beat in eggs.
2—Blend with pineapple and syrup.
3—Cut bread into cubes and add to mixture.
4—Pour entire mixture into 9" x 13" pan.
5—Bake 350° for 50–60 minutes or until a knife into center comes away clean.
Hot Kugle is tempting when served with dinner.
Warm Kugle is delicious when served with a whipped topping after dinner.
Cold Kugle is satisfying when served as a snack.

Fondue with Croutons
Fondue is a tasty serve-yourself hot dish—a party food with easy clean up.

Savory Fondue—Melt sharp-cheeses and serve with toasted white and/or dark croutons and long handle forks for dipping. For mealtime excitement, serve cheese fondue—with white or dark croutons and a salad for dinner.

Sweet Fondue—Substitute chocolate for cheese. Melt chocolate and serve with sweetbread croutons and long handled forks for dipping. Serve melted chocolate with sweetbread croutons for dessert.

Soup and Croutons
Utensils—four-ovenproof serving bowls
Ingredients—soup—homemade, packaged or can—for four, 1-cup croutons, ½-cup grated Parmesan cheese

1—Pour heated soup into ovenproof serving bowls.
2—Sprinkle soup with cheese and place croutons on top.
3—Sprinkle croutons with cheese, and place under broiler until brown.
Have a stress break with high nutrition soup and 15 minutes quiet time.

Stuffing
Caution: Dieters and Nutrition Experts—High Fat Area
Stuffing can be made with bread, crackers or cornmeal, and with celery, onions, mushrooms, chestnuts, sausage, oysters, dry fruit and whatever.

This stuffing recipe is made with cubed white bread that is 3–4 days old, butter, onions, celery, salt, parsley, and poultry seasoning, and it serves eight people. Double or triple the recipe for holiday sampling, and leftovers. Because this stuffing contains no meat, it can be prepared a day or two before required.

Do not put stuffing into turkey/chicken/duck until ready to place into the oven. When combined for too long either in the refrigerator or at room temperature, bread and meat juice breed bacteria.

Utensils—large pot 14–16 qt, large spoon
Ingredients—two loaves Basic white or 28–30-slices of bread, 1½-cup butter or margarine, 2-cups onions, 2-cups celery, ¼-cup chopped parsley, 1-tea-

spoon salt, ¾-cup warm water, 1-tablespoon poultry seasoning (marjoram, thyme, nutmeg, sage, rosemary, pepper)

1—Place bread slices on a tray and in an out-of-the-way area (top of refrigerator) for 24 hours.
Turn bread once or so to dry both sides—if too soft, dry bread in oven at 200°.
The bread should be dry but not crisp.
2—With a sharp knife, cut bread into 1" x 1" cubes.
(Place four or five slices atop each other and cut through.)
3—Melt butter in the large pot over low heat.
4—Into melted butter place onion and celery and cook on low heat.
5—When celery and onions are tender, turn off heat.
6—Stir in salt, parsley, poultry seasoning and warm water.
7—Add all the bread cubes and stir to absorb melted mixture.
8—Use a large spoon to bring this together. If too dry, add a little more warm water.
9—Stuff fowl, chicken/turkey/duck, shortly before placing into the oven. Bake fowl as directed.
10—Pack remaining stuffing into bread pans. Bake bread pan stuffing about an hour in 350° oven.
The bread pan should fit on the shelf with the poultry.
11—When cooked, mix stuffing from fowl with stuffing from bread pan. This provides a delicious mixture of soft moist stuffing from the fowl and bits of crisp stuffing from the top of bread pan.

The good aroma will bring family to the kitchen for taste testing. Stand guard. Keep in cool area until ready to use and away from samplers.

♥ *December 1961—As a new cook Richard, Ed's childhood friend, had to unexpectedly prepare Christmas dinner when his mother took sick. He purchased a turkey, pre packaged stuffing etc. He was pleased with his effort. When the turkey was baked and the stuffing removed, so too was a little bag holding turkey neck, heart, liver and gizzard. At the dinner table Richard and his mother had a good laugh about the bag of turkey parts that butchers include for gravy making.*

♥ *If you chop onions with a slice of bread in your mouth, your eyes will not tear. You look the fool, but it works.*

Breadcrumbs

When Basic white, sweet or dark bread is a few days old, make breadcrumbs. Place bread slices on a rack where air can circulate for about 24 hours. For pure white breadcrumbs remove the crust before drying. If dark crumbs are not a bother, dry the crust too. Stale bread makes stale tasting breadcrumbs.

Breadcrumb Recipe

Oven—200°
Time—according to dryness of bread
Utensils—baking sheet, grater, rolling pin or food chopper
Ingredients—3–4 days old bread slices—white, sweet or dark
One slice of bread will make about ½ cup loosely placed crumbs.

1—Place bread on baking sheet in a preheated 200° oven.
2—Heat until dry enough to crumble—not toasted/watch closely.
3—Use a grater, rolling pin, blender or food chopper to crumb dried bread.
Home baked breadcrumbs have no preservative, store in freezer.
Sweet breads brown faster than non-sweet breads—watch closely.

Breadcrumbs/Au Gratin

Add ¼ cup cheese to 1-cup breadcrumbs, and top hot cooked casserole with breadcrumbs and brown under broiler.

Breadcrumb Topping

Utensils—fry pan
Ingredients—¾-cups breadcrumbs, 4-tablespoons butter

1—Melt butter and add breadcrumbs.
2—Cook until butter and crumbs are brown—watch closely.
Place atop steamed vegetables or baked casserole.

Breadcrumbs and Cauliflower

Breadcrumb Topping makes steamed cauliflower a dish worth serving. First cook cauliflower in boiling water until a fork will insert with ease into underside. Then place whole cauliflower in a serving dish and top with Breadcrumb Topping.

Breadcrumbs Seasoned
Mild breadcrumbs: 3-cups Basic white breadcrumbs and 2-tablespoons dried parsley
Tangy breadcrumbs: 3-cups Basic dark breadcrumbs and 1-teaspoon oregano and ¼-teaspoon garlic salt
Sweet-breadcrumbs: 3-cups Basic sweet breadcrumbs and pinch cinnamon or nutmeg

Breadcrumbs for soup
To thicken soup, add ½-cup breadcrumbs. As the soup continues to cooks, the crumbs will disappear and the soup will thicken.

Casserole with Breadcrumbs
Top baked casserole with breadcrumbs, dot with butter and place back into the oven. The buttered breadcrumbs will be brown, crisp and tasty.

For a happy flutter, feed birds home baked bread

7

Reflecting On Your Diet

This chapter in alphabetic order—Brewers Yeast, Calories, Carbohydrates, Cholesterol, Fat, Fiber-Dietary, Gluten, Minerals, Protein, Sodium, Salt, Stress, Vitamins

What wholesome food can all age group enjoy every day, every meal, every snack? You guessed it—home baked bread.

Home baked bread can be made without artificial coloring, saturated fats, sodium or preservatives (except those found in purchased ingredients). And homemade bread can be made with additional vitamins, minerals and dietary fiber. Follow the Basic bread recipes, and become comfortable with the directions. After you are comfortable, consider altering ingredients to suit your diet.

If your diet requires extra protein or less sodium, check Chapter 5 Ingredients that Change Taste and Texture, for the ingredient with more/less protein/sodium, and adjust the Basic bread recipe accordingly.

The vitamin and mineral information shown in this book is from U. S. Government Nutritive Value of Foods and from individual product packages.

♥*November 11th 1991—The New York Times (NYT) printed my reply to an article "The Joy of Old" by Charles Rembar. His advice was to ignore middle age and go directly to old age. My reply to the NYT, "After 55, good health is young. Poor health is old. There are no stages."*

Brewers Yeast

Brewers yeast is a natural source of B complex vitamins. Since Brewers Yeast is not a living yeast cell, it cannot be substituted for active dry yeast. It can be added to dry ingredients for additional protein. Brewers yeast has a strong flavor. Start with 1-tablespoon brewers yeast per 4-cups flour.

	Calories	Carbohydrate	Fat	Protein	Sodium	Fiber
1-tablespoon	25	3	trace	3 g	10 mg	0

Calories

A calorie is a measure of energy. If you eat more calories/energy than your body requires, then your body stores the excess in body fat. Home baked bread can be low or high in calories. As the baker you decide.

Although folks eat in restaurants more often than in years past, a U. S. Government survey shows that 70% of calories are from foods eaten at home or carried for lunch.

The average American eats the equivalent of 20-teaspoons sugar a day. A 12-fluid-ounce cola drink contains about 9-teaspoons sugar. There are 16-calories in 1-teaspoon of sugar and 35-calories in 1-teaspoon fat.

Calories-

¼-cup	package	teaspoon	¼ cup	¼ cup	¼ cup	one
Flour	Yeast	Salt	Sugar	Milk	Vegetable oil	Egg
100	20	0	192	38	480	75

All-purpose flour has 100 calories per ¼ cup, and 100% whole-wheat flour has 130 calories per ¼ cup.

♦ To decrease calories, use less sugar and oil, and substitute water for milk.
♦ To increase calories, stay with the Basic recipe, and substitute whole milk for water and add fruit, nuts and cheese

Carbohydrate

Carbohydrates are our main energy source: sugar and starch are our main carbo-hydrate source. There are three types of carbohydrates:

Simple carbohydrates—fruit/sugar

Complex carbohydrates—whole grains/starch

Refined/processed carbohydrates—cakes and cookies/sugar and starch

Carbohydrates-

¼-cup	package	teaspoon	¼ cup	¼ cup	¼ cup	one
Flour	Yeast	Salt	Sugar	Milk	Vegetable oil	Egg
22 g	3 g	0	48 g	2 g	0	1 g

All-purpose flour has 22 g per ¼ cup, 100% whole-wheat flour has 26 g per ¼ cup.

♦ Basic sweet bread made with eggs, honey, dried fruit and nuts is an enjoyable addition to a high carbohydrate diet.

♦ Fifty to sixty percent of our daily calories should be from carbohydrates.

♦ Too many carbohydrates can make you tired. To soothe your system and help you to sleep, try home baked bread with honey and a warm beverage.

Cholesterol

Cholesterol, a waxy substance, is present in all body parts, including the nervous system, muscle, skin, liver, intestines, and heart. The body makes enough choles-terol to meet its needs. Cholesterol is used in the manufacture of hormones, bile acid, and vitamin D.

Blood Cholesterol is cholesterol circulating in the bloodstream. It is made in the liver and absorbed from the food we eat. The blood carries cholesterol for use by all parts of the body. A high level of blood cholesterol leads to arteriosclerosis and an increased risk of heart disease.

Dietary Cholesterol is cholesterol in the food we eat. It is present in animal ori-gin food, and not plant origin. Not all cholesterol is bad for you. But dietary cho-lesterol, like dietary saturated fat, raises blood cholesterol, which increases the risk for heart disease.

HDL's (High-density Lipoprotein)—HDL's are lipoproteins that contain a small amount of cholesterol and carry cholesterol away from body cells and tissues to the liver for excretion from the body. A low level of HDL increases the risk of heart disease, so the higher the HDL level, the better. HDL is sometimes called the "good" cholesterol.

LDL's (Low-density Lipoprotein)—LDL's are lipoproteins that contain most of the cholesterol in the blood. LDL, the 'bad' cholesterol, carries cholesterol to the tissues of the body including the arteries. For this reason, a high level of LDL increases the risk of heart disease.

Trans fatty acids lower good HDL and raises bad LDL. Trans fatty acid is formed when oil is hydrogenated into a semi solid state such as oil in some margarine.

Cholesterol-

¼-cup	1-package	1-teaspoon	¼-cup	¼-cup	¼-cup	one
Flour	Yeast	Salt	Sugar	Milk	Vegetable oil	Egg
0	0	0	0	9 mg	0	180 mg

There is no cholesterol in ¼-cup flour—all-purpose or 100% whole wheat.

♦ There is no cholesterol in flour.
♦ There is no cholesterol in vegetable oil, which is recommended in Basic bread recipes.
♦ Eggs are high in cholesterol. One egg yolk has ten times as much cholesterol as an ounce of meat.
♦ A slice of 100% whole wheat bread with jelly is a cholesterol-free treat.
♦ One tablespoon of butter has 30 mg cholesterol

♥ *1992—We celebrate Easter Sunday with a brunch. And because my brunch-foods are high in cholesterol, I decided not to include cinnamon buns. Daniel noticed that cinnamon buns were missing from the brunch table, and when I told him why. He suggested, "You make the food selection, and the family will worry about the cholesterol."*

Fat

Fat works with carbohydrates to give energy to our body, and fat works with protein for continuous cell-growth. Because fat is good for you, the American Heart Association recommends 30 g of fat per day.

For weight loss, when your grocery shop think high fiber/low fat and low calories. When eating out, think bread, not butter. A product that says 'cholesterol-free' can still contain fat. For example a manufacturer label states that that peanut butter is cholesterol-free, but 1 tablespoon has 8 grams of fat. Check product label for nutrition information.

Fats are

Polyunsaturated—corn, safflower, sesame, soybean, and sunflower
Monosaturated—olive, peanut
Saturated—solid at room temperature
Unsaturated—liquid at room temperature: vegetable, safflower, corn, soybean, and olive oil (Nuts and seeds have unsaturated fat, which is the good-for-you fat.)
Soluble—not cooked out of food; they are retained by our body
Water soluble—cooked out of food thus not retained by our body
Hydrogenated—vegetable oils are hydrogenated to make them solid (margarine) at room temperature: lard, butter, coconut, and palm

Fat-

¼-cup	1-package	1-teaspoon	¼-cup	¼-cup	¼-cup	one
Flour	Yeast	Salt	Sugar	Milk	Vegetable oil	Egg
0	trace	0	0	2 g	56 g	5 g

There is 1 g fat in ¼-cup 100% whole-wheat flour.
♦ For low fat energy pick up, drizzle honey on croutons that are prepared without butter.
♦ There is no fat in ¼ cup white flour.
♦ To decrease fat in Basic recipes, omit vegetable oil and use skim milk.
♦ Bread can be made without oil and without milk.

Fiber-Dietary

Dietary fiber is a fine, tasteless, odorless strand found in nuts, seeds, grains, fruits and vegetables. Dietary fiber has no nutritional value. Dietary fiber is bulk, cellulose, and roughage and it is necessary for our well-being. Normal food digestion depends on dietary fiber, yet modern food processing removes most dietary fiber. Insoluble dietary fiber such as whole grains and skins cannot be dissolved in water. Insoluble dietary fiber promotes regularity. Soluble dietary fiber as in apple juice is liquefied.

Most Americans do not get enough fiber to realize its potential benefits. The typical American eats about 11 grams of fiber a day, according to the American Dietetic Association. And, The U. S. Government recommends fiber amount per day is 25–35 grams for most people.
♦ For mealtime and snack time, children, teenagers, seniors, expecting mothers and those with special needs should eat 100% whole grain bread, which is high in fiber.

Dietary fiber-

¼-cup	1-package	1-teaspoon	¼-cup	¼-cup	¼-cup	one
Flour	Yeast	Salt	Sugar	Milk	Vegetable oil	Egg
0	0	0	0	0	0	0

All-purpose flour has 0 fiber in ¼ cup, 100% whole-wheat flour has 4 g fiber in ¼ cup.

We digest food from mouth to esophagus to stomach.
While food is in the stomach, enzymes help break down the food. Food then settles in the small intestine where digestive fluids assist waste from pancreas, liver and gall bladder on into the colon. Waste material can stay too long in the colon and become dry, which can lead to problems. It can take a few days to complete this process.

We do not digest fiber rather fiber absorbs water and gives bulk to waste material. Consequently we eliminate waste material more often and with greater ease. Because bran is high in fiber, bran works well as a laxative. Many adults take fiber supplements. If a diet includes sufficient water, whole grains, nuts and fresh and/ or dried fruits, then fiber supplements can be avoided.

The U. S. Government recommends increasing liquid and fiber in our diet, thus waste material will not remain in the colon too long and cause constipation. Fiber has been called the alternative medicine for constipation.

Fiber
♦ Because fiber absorbs water in greater quantities, Basic dark high fiber bread provides a full feeling.
♦ Grains such as oat, rye and wheat and seeds such as sesame, flax and poppy are high in fiber.
♦ Fresh or dried fruit with skin such as raisins, apricots and dates are high in fiber.
♦ Foods with a high fiber content take longer to chew and swallow.
♦ Whole grains used in bread baking are high in water absorbing fiber.
♦ For early morning nutrition, consider Basic white bread, dry fruit, nuts and a warm beverage.
♦ For late night nutrition, snack on Basic dark bread and warm beverage.
♦ Fiber has the ability to absorb many times its own weight in water.
♦ Fiber gives bread density, takes longer to chew and gives one a full feeling.
♦ Basic 100% whole grain bread is recommended for those who wish to lose weight.
♦ A dieter's hunger can be eased for longer periods with high fiber foods.

Fiber/Flour Experiment
To check the fiber in white flour vs. 100% whole wheat flour—
First, take ¼ cup white flour and pour ¾-cup water on top.
After 20 minutes, white flour will set on top, congealing like a gummy mass.
White flour has less than one-gram fiber per ¼-cup flour.
Next, take ¼ cup 100% whole-wheat flour and pour ¾-cup water on top.
After 20 minutes, 100% whole-wheat flour will absorb the liquid and double in size.
100% whole-wheat flour has 4 g fiber per ¼-cup flour.

Although we do not eat flour by the ¼-cup full, there is about ¼-cups flour in one Basic white bread slice. For high fiber bread, consider adding bran, wheat germ, fruit and/or nuts to the Basic white, sweet or dark recipe.

♥ *2003—Exercise is important to good health, and I enjoy walking. On an early morning walk, in my small town, I became aware of a car slowly moving along behind me. After a bit, I stopped and when the car slowed down beside me, I questioned, "Are you having a problem?" The driver replied, "Well no, I want to deliver the newspaper, but don't want to pull the car up in front of you."*

Minerals

Bread ingredients are a natural source of minerals. Some minerals are in trace amounts.

(See vitamins)

Fruit, nuts and seeds contribute additional minerals to bread goodness.

Minerals	Natural Source
Calcium	egg, dairy, molasses, whole grains
Chlorine	salt
Cobalt	dairy
Chromium	corn oil, whole grains
Copper	whole grains
Fluorine	water
Iodine	iodized salt
Iron	eggs, molasses, whole grains
Magnesium	whole grains
Manganese	eggs, whole grains
Molybdenum	whole grains
Nickel	whole grains,
Phosphorus	dairy, whole grains
Selenium	dairy, whole grains
Sodium	salt
Sulfur	eggs
Vanadium	vegetable oil
Zinc	whole grains

Protein

We cannot survive without proteins—they are vital for our mental and physical well-being.

Proteins are complete and incomplete.
Complete proteins are found in animal foods: milk, eggs and meat.
Incomplete proteins are found in natural ingredients—vegetables, fruits, grains, and beans. Proteins are limiting and essential chains of amino acids. The amino acids chains are 22 in number; each has its own name and use within our body. We require all 22 for good health.

Protein-

¼-cup	1-package	1-teaspoon	¼ cup	¼-cup	¼-cup	one
Flour	Yeast	Salt	Sugar	Milk	Vegetable oil	Egg
3 g	3 g	0	0	2 g	0	6 g

All-purpose flour has 3 g protein in ¼-cup, and 100% whole wheat flour has 5 g protein in ¼-cup

Protein

♦ For high protein bread, add ingredients such as amaranth flour, brewers yeast, cottage cheese, gluten, groundnuts, powder milk, or soy flour. Refer Chapter 5—Ingredients that Change Bread Taste and Texture for suggested amounts to use in bread baking.
♦ White bread made with the addition of soy flour and soymilk is an excellent addition to a high protein diet.
♦ Individuals who cannot digest high protein flour purchase bread made from gluten free flour. See Gluten in Chapter 5—Ingredients That Change Bread Taste and Texture.

Sodium/Salt

Sodium is a mineral that is necessary for our well-being. Salt is a natural compound composed of 40% sodium and 60% chloride. Research has shown, that too much sodium can contribute to high blood pressure. Sodium is a food preservative and flavor-enhancer found in bread spreads: margarine, mustard, mayonnaise, catsup and most packaged foods. Check the product label.

Sodium-

¼-cup	1-package	1-teaspoon	¼-cup	¼-cup	¼-cup	one
Flour	Yeast	Salt	Sugar	Milk	Vegetable oil	Egg
0	4 mg	2,300 mg	0	30 mg	0	63 mg

There is no sodium in ¼-cup all-purpose flour or 100% whole-wheat flour.

♦There are 1,000-milligrams in 1 gram sodium; most labels show sodium in milligrams (mg).

♦There are 2,000-mg sodium in 1-teaspoon salt.

♦The recommended sodium/salt amount per day is one teaspoon or 2,000-mg.

♦A recipe in a book published 100 years ago recommended 1-tablespoon salt per three cups flour. The Basic white, sweet and dark recipe suggests 2-teaspoons salt per four cups flour.

Vitamins
Bread ingredients are a natural source of vitamins. Some vitamins are in trace amounts. (See minerals) And fruit, nuts and seeds contribute additional vitamins to bread goodness.

Vitamin	Natural Source
Vitamin A	eggs, dairy, whole grains
B 1 (Thiamin)	eggs, dairy, whole grains
B 2 (Riboflavin)	eggs, dairy, whole grains
B 3 (Niacin)	dairy, whole grains
B 5 (Pantothenic Acid)	eggs, whole grains
B 6 (Pyridoxine)	eggs, dairy, whole grains
B 12 (Cyanocobalomin)	eggs, dairy, whole grains
Folic Acid	whole grains
Choline	whole grains, eggs
Inositol	dairy, whole grains, yeast
Methionine	eggs, dairy
Biotin	eggs
PABA	molasses, whole grains
C	dairy
D	dairy
E	eggs, soy, whole grains
K	eggs
F	corn oil

♥ *Raising a family is hectic, going to work is exhausting and retirement is busy. To reduce stress, consider baking bread. Concentrate on kneading dough. Pay attention to dough rising. Smell the bread baking. Enjoy warm bread with cold butter. Share home-baked bread with family and friends.*

♥ *Hopefully the recipes in this bread book will help you to be successful with three Basic recipes: white, sweet, and dark.*

Hopefully the recipes suggestions will encourage you to try your hand at substituting ingredients. And—
Hopefully the selected ♥ notes from my journal will inspire you to keep a journal.

Bake Bread to Nourish the Body, Energize the Mind and Soothe the Soul.

—The End—

About the Author

I have been baking interesting and nutritious breads since the 1960s. Bread plays a major role in my life: bread baking, bread eating, recipe reading, writing and teaching.

Index

0-595-33021-5

CPSIA information can be obtained
at www.ICGtesting.com
Printed in the USA
BVHW030146131119
563690BV00001B/25/P